How to survive and succeed
as a teaching assistant

Veronica Birkett

Acknowledgements

The author would like to thank the following for their support and commitment:

- Nazima Khan and Jo Blyton of Broadwater Primary School, Wandsworth, London;
- Shelley Birkins and Luke Spillington of Ash Lea Special School, Cotgrave, Nottingham;
- the numerous TAs she has encountered who have gone through the HLTA process and have won her admiration for their knowledge, tenacity and determination;
- TAs everywhere for the valuable contribution they are making to the education of our children;
- two great editors, Debbie Pullinger and Sadie Hiblin, whose combined skills have made this book what it is.

How to survive and succeed as a Teaching Assistant
MT10768
ISBN-13: 978 1 85503 430 3

© Veronica Birkett
Illustration © Robin Edmonds
All rights reserved
First published 2001
Second edition published 2008

Printed in the UK for LDA
Abbeygate House, East Road, Cambridge, CB1 1DB, UK

Contents

Contents

Introduction

The first edition of this book was written six years ago, and since then there have been vast changes in education which have had significant implications for teaching assistants (TAs). This book has been fully revised and updated to reflect those changes. More and more children with special educational needs (SEN) are being educated in mainstream schools; and in order to support these children effectively increasing numbers of well-trained, qualified TAs are needed. Ever more demanding government initiatives have been introduced; TAs are shouldering more responsibility and teachers have much higher expectations of them and their role. In addition, the national agreement on remodelling the school workforce has led to the development of new and more responsible roles for TAs. Higher level teaching assistant (HLTA) status provides opportunities for better qualified TAs to teach whole classes in collaboration with teachers, and to take on a range of additional responsibilities.

This new edition includes information on recent changes in SEN provision as well as about the new qualifications and training for TAs. Several new sections have been added, including a chapter on liaising effectively with other staff and troubleshooting tips on what to do if you don't feel supported. It will help you understand and appreciate your job as a TA, leaving you feeling more motivated and able to succeed. This book will help you to appreciate that a TA's job can be challenging, and also rewarding and enjoyable.

This book is ideal for you if any of the following apply to you:
- ❍ you are considering becoming a TA and want to know more about what the job entails;
- ❍ you are new to the TA role and want reassuring, practical advice so you feel knowledgeable, confident, and well prepared for your role in the classroom;
- ❍ you are an experienced TA who is looking for information on how to work more effectively with pupils or colleagues in school or who is finding some aspects of the job challenging and looking for further support, or who wants to take a fresh look at the job and feel newly inspired;
- ❍ you are a TA with two years' experience or more who wants to know more about HLTA status, what it involves and how to acquire it;
- ❍ you are a teacher, head teacher or special educational needs co-ordinator (SENCo) who would like to work more effectively with TAs and wish to view the job from a TA's perspective – if so, you will also be interested in reading *How to Support and Manage Teaching Assistants* by the same author.

Chapter 1
The role of teaching assistants

An evolving role

The role of the TA has evolved greatly over the years. It is only relatively recently that the job has become more clearly defined, with a formalisation of qualifications, pay and career structure. My own teaching career began in the 1960s and the only adults who gave me practical help then were the chosen few invited to accompany the class on the annual school trip, or who helped out at Christmas parties. That was it. Welfare assistants had been employed in special schools for some time, but the presence of additional adults in mainstream classrooms was virtually unknown.

In the 1980s things began to change. When I returned to teaching, having taken time off to raise my three daughters, I was allocated an adult – known as an ancillary – one afternoon a week to help in my class. I was surprised and slightly puzzled. What was I supposed to do with her? It didn't take me long to decide. Basically, all the things I wasn't good at or keen on myself! Putting up wall displays, mixing paints, sorting out children's work … and, if anyone in my class had the misfortune to be sick, well …! When I was stuck for jobs to keep her occupied, she would take children out, one by one, to hear them read. After a while I began to wonder how I had managed for so many years without this extra support. These classroom ancillaries had no training and no official job description. Had there been one, it might have looked like this.

Job description

Willing, cheerful and hard-working person required to:

- ⊙ put up wall displays and take down wall displays
- ⊙ make and deliver cups of tea at specified times to teachers
- ⊙ wash up cups of said teachers
- ⊙ mix paints
- ⊙ clean up pupils after accidents and stick plasters on cuts
- ⊙ carry out playground duties
- ⊙ ring the bell
- ⊙ tidy out the art cupboard
- ⊙ remove staples from display board
- ⊙ hear pupils read, again and again and again, and again

"Would a cup of tea help at all?"

I should like to thank all those classroom ancillaries who helped transform children's artwork into wonderful displays; brought me cups of tea on cold, cheerless mornings; and comforted me in times of stress with soothing words, encouragement and kindness. Their work was truly appreciated, just like that of the current TAs. The nature of the job has changed since I first worked in schools, and as a TA you will have a very different role now. There is far less paint-mixing and card-cutting, and far more involvement with teaching and learning.

Why things changed

The introduction of a National Curriculum for all schools following the Education Reform Act of 1988 had a radical effect on general classroom practice. It provided the government with a means of assessing standards in schools and emphasised the need to raise standards overall. Standard attainment targets (SATs) tests were introduced, revealing how many pupils were working at a level deemed appropriate for their age. It became easier to identify which schools were working successfully, and which were not. Schools became accountable because there were now national statistics available on which to judge them. More TAs began to be employed at this time to help schools raise standards.

The 1993 Education Act, followed by the introduction of the Code of Practice on the identification and assessment of SEN in 1994, introduced further significant changes in the number, status and work of classroom assistants. Like the National Curriculum, the Code introduced a national framework and provided guidance for schools in making appropriate provision for pupils with SEN. Schools began to employ additional TAs, for schools were expected to take far more account of pupils with SEN and include many more pupils in mainstream schools, and to do that they would need additional support. In 1998 the government's Programme for Action underlined their drive to include more pupils with SEN in mainstream schools, and this provided even more job opportunities for TAs.

So, the ever increasing number of TAs working in schools since the early 1990s have tended to provide either:

● general classroom support, to help raise standards – the presence of TAs also helps support struggling pupils and may prevent the occurrence of a special need;

● support for pupils with SEN in accordance with the policy of inclusion.

The job today

Because of the changes in the TA's role, schools should have two separate job descriptions, one for TAs who have a general role of support and the other for those who are employed specifically to work with SEN pupils. There will be some overlap between these jobs as you will often encounter SEN pupils when providing general classroom assistance, and when working with a child with SEN you will rarely do so solely in a one-to-one situation. The job description is important. It is a form of agreement that clarifies what the school expects from the TA. When you take on the role, you are agreeing to the particular duties outlined in your job description. If further duties are requested which you are not happy with and are not included in the job description, you have the right to question them.

My job has given me the opportunity to develop my knowledge in so many areas.

Job description for TA employed to provide general support

Purpose

To work with and support members of the teaching staff in ensuring that pupils receive the highest possible standards of care and education, becoming safe, secure and successful.

Duties

Working within established guidelines to support the teacher in:

- ⊙ ensuring that pupils are safe;
- ⊙ teaching the planned curriculum;
- ⊙ using resources effectively;
- ⊙ producing and maintaining a welcoming and stimulating classroom environment;
- ⊙ encouraging pupils to work and play independently;
- ⊙ evaluating and planning children's work;
- ⊙ maintaining strong home–school links.

The TA should also:

- ⊙ be involved in planning and taking the initiative to ensure that they understand the lesson objective before teaching begins;
- ⊙ evaluate designated teaching activities and feed back to class teacher;
- ⊙ assist in national and school-based assessment arrangements, such as SATs, Year 3 Literacy Support, GCSEs;
- ⊙ meet regularly with class teachers to plan work and raise or resolve concerns.

Job description for TA employed to work with pupils with SEN or a statement

Purpose

To support named children who are protected by a statement of SEN or who are in need of additional support owing to learning or other difficulties.

Special conditions

⦿ The TA will work under the guidance of the SENCo, head teacher and appropriate class teachers.

⦿ The TA will be made aware of the relevant contents of the statement of SEN, if a pupil has one.

⦿ The TA will be familiar with the pupil's individual education plan (IEP).

Main responsibilities

⦿ To support the child in all areas of the curriculum, as directed by the class teacher.

⦿ To support the child as a member of a collaborative group.

⦿ To help the child develop social and organisational skills.

⦿ To monitor the child's work and keep appropriate records.

⦿ To carry out programmes of work devised to meet the child's specific needs.

⦿ To assist in the planning of activities to attain the above functions.

⦿ To prepare appropriate materials.

⦿ To minister to the physical needs of the child with reference to guidance on first aid in schools and the school policy on the administration of medicines.

⦿ To liaise with parents and professionals.

⦿ To work within the general aims of the school, and to contribute to the overall ethos of the school.

⦿ To undertake any related activities appropriate to working with the child, as directed by the head teacher or SENCo.

Working with Teaching Assistants: a Good Practice Guide (DfES 2000) is a useful source of further information on what a TA's job entails.

Obviously, your role will depend very much on the type of school in which you are employed. You may be asked to:

- work with pupils in a reception class, which will involve very different responsibilities from those called for in a secondary school;
- support a group of pupils whose knowledge of the English language is limited and who need support to participate fully in the class;
- support gifted and able pupils;
- work in particular areas of the curriculum;
- work with individual pupils with specific and complex needs;
- work in special schools or in behaviour or learning support units attached to mainstream schools;
- work with sick children in hospital.

Your role will depend on why the school employed you, and what its priorities are, as well as on your own preferences. If you are working with children with SEN, their physical and/or learning needs will dictate your role to some extent.

Supporting pupils

You may be working with pupils in a whole-class situation, in groups or as individuals.

Whole class

As a TA you may be involved in:

- adapting materials to support pupils in different areas of the curriculum;
- preparing equipment for art, science, cooking, and so on;
- accompanying children, with teachers, on school trips/visits;
- looking after the library;
- making resources and worksheets;
- first aid;
- working with pupils on computers;
- accompanying children who are accommodated in special units to classes in mainstream schools;
- attending swimming sessions with teacher and children;
- attending review meetings;
- attending literacy/numeracy planning sessions;
- supporting pupils in literacy/numeracy lessons;
- supporting pupils across all areas of the curriculum, particularly in secondary schools.

I like the opportunity to meet new people every day. I had no idea when I started how much I would have to do with other adults. I thought it would be just me and a child all day.

I enjoy the variety of tasks I am asked to carry out – no two days are the same.

I have always liked books, so for this reason the head asked me to be in charge of the library. I jumped at the chance!

I just like being in the company of children. I like the things they say and do. They say such lovely things.

The groups I have are too large.

Groups

The teacher will select the pupils with whom you work. The selection will depend on your job description and why you have been employed in the first instance, as well as on the needs of the class teacher at the time. You may work with groups of pupils in a number of ways:

● You may be asked to support a group of low-ability pupils; your job may be to consolidate work from a previous literacy or numeracy lesson using an activity prepared by the teacher.

● You may be asked to support a group of high achievers in order to provide more challenging work, beyond the capacity of most of the class.

● TAs have been involved in implementing many DfES-driven initiatives (now the Department for Children, Schools and Families – DCSF) aimed at raising standards. You may help with Year 3 Literacy Support or Early Literacy Support (ELS) programmes, both designed for children who have fallen behind in literacy.

● You may be working with a group of pupils for whom English is an additional language (EAL), and who need language support to enable them to access the curriculum fully. If so, you will probably receive some training in teaching English as an additional language. If you can speak the first language of any EAL pupils in your school, you may be called upon to assist them.

● You may also be asked to deliver particular programmes of work for which you would need prior training from relevant professionals. For example, some dyspraxic pupils may benefit from a motor-skills programme or there may be dyslexic pupils who need a structured programme devised to address their needs. Alternatively, you may help to run a social-skills group for children struggling with interpersonal and communication skills.

● If you find there are any behaviour problems in your group, do let the class teacher know. If the problem is particularly pervasive, behaviour management training may be helpful. There is more information on this in Chapter 3.

Individuals

You may provide support for individual pupils. Such focused support may be necessary for a variety of reasons, but the usual one is that a pupil has been identified as having an SEN. Pupils with SEN are provided with an individual education plan (IEP) which contains about four learning and/or behaviour targets. They may be receiving School Action support – which means they have an IEP and support provided within the school – or they may be placed at School Action Plus. The latter means that the school has sufficient concern to involve an outside professional with the pupil. Some pupils have statements; they will have been allocated the support of a TA for a set number of hours a week. (For more information on IEPs and SEN, see Chapter 5.) The role of the TA is to support the pupil in the achievement of their IEP targets. Occasionally it is appropriate to work individually with the pupil. For example, a pupil may have an IEP with learning goals specific to them which are not relevant to any other pupil. This might apply to a pupil with severe language difficulties who has a programme devised by a speech and language therapist, or to a dyspraxic pupil who has a daily exercise programme.

When working with a pupil with a statement, you are funded by the local authority (LA), or by the school if the SEN money has been devolved to schools. If the pupil makes progress to the extent that they no longer need a statement or your support, your time will be withdrawn and you may be out of a job. Don't worry if that happens. You will have gained valuable experience and should find yourself in demand, perhaps to work with a different pupil in the same school. The fact that one particular pupil no longer needs you is a matter of celebration. It's a bit like when children grow up and leave home – it's a time for celebration and sadness.

Your role with an individual pupil may involve offering support across the curriculum. For example, a pupil with physical problems may need help in PE, while a pupil with a severe visual impairment may need your full-time support in every lesson. It's often important to be aware of the focus of the lesson beforehand so you can be adequately prepared.

If you are supporting a pupil with severe and complex needs across the curriculum, you may be involved in:

- preparing resources such as word banks and visual timetables or enlarging worksheets;
- accompanying the child to the toilet;
- supervising the child in the playground at lunchtime;
- checking equipment (e.g. hearing aids, wheelchairs);
- carrying out exercise programmes under supervision.

If you are allocated a specific SEN pupil to work with, it may be appropriate, at times, to work with them in a group situation. The stimulation of group work is important, but if you find the group selected is distracting you from meeting the needs of your pupil, discuss this with the teacher. It's important to ensure that the group is working at around the same level as your pupil.

Whatever the situation, you should receive support and guidance from the class teacher, the SENCo and possibly an outside professional. They should all advise you on targets to work towards with the child as well as resources and teaching strategies to use.

Supporting teachers

Working with the teacher to support pupils' learning and behaviour is the main way in which you, as a TA, may be occupied. This work includes assisting teachers with differentiation – making the curriculum accessible to all pupils, whatever their ability. Many pupils, particularly in primary schools, are in mixed-ability classes, so ensuring that work is appropriate to the level of ability is crucial. Work may be differentiated in several ways.

Differentiation

By support: You may be asked to give direct support to pupils by sitting with a small group or an individual to offer encouragement or advice, to answer questions or to help with spellings. This type of support should also be available to higher-ability pupils.

I find it hard to cope with children with different abilities in the same group. I need more help in finding suitable resources for all of them.

cloze text with words missing

By task: For groups of pupils in mixed-ability classes, it may be appropriate for the teacher to assign different tasks to each ability group. For example, if a class is working on volcanoes, the high-ability group may work more independently and go to the library to carry out research. Those of average ability could answer questions from a worksheet on volcanoes. The low-ability group could complete a cloze procedure activity, whereby they fill in the blank words on a sheet summarising what causes volcanoes.

By time: The teacher may set similar learning objectives for the whole class, but allow some groups more time to complete an activity.

By outcome: This simply means that all pupils will be working on the same task, but the teacher – and you as the TA – are aware that the standard of the finished work will differ according to the ability of the pupils.

Well, at least the kinaesthetic learners enjoyed it ...!

Thanks Miss, that was great

By resources: The resources selected in order to complete a specific task may vary from group to group. Some groups may require specific word lists to help them accomplish a writing task independently, while another group are able to use a dictionary.

By learning styles: Everybody has a preference about how they best learn, receive and retain information. To ensure that all learning styles are catered for, teachers adopt a range of presentation techniques, use different resources, and set different work. There are, broadly speaking, three types of learner:
  • *Visual learners:* They tend to remember what they see, so they prefer looking at information presented visually, such as maps or diagrams, and watching demonstrations and DVDs.
  • *Auditory learners*: They are more likely to remember what they hear, so they favour learning through discussions, sharing work with others or reading aloud.
  • *Kinaesthetic learners:* They respond best to movement, so they like practical, hands-on activities such as making a model or performing a role-play.

Providing resources for the kinaesthetic learner may be the biggest challenge, and when working as a TA you may be allocated to work with these learners, helping them by offering a more practical approach.

Additional ways of supporting the teacher

I like it when the teacher trusts me enough to use my own initiative when I'm working with a group of children.

You may be asked to support the teacher by assisting on visits out of school or by taking on a number of routine tasks. These include preparing resources, helping with wall displays, photocopying, and accompanying pupils to the school library or computer room. In addition, TAs with HLTA status (see Chapter 2) offer support by relieving the teacher of class responsibilities, teaching the class for a specific time to enable them to carry out planning and administrative duties.

The reality check
Your TA role may involve any of the following tasks:
- helping put coats on
- helping take coats off
- helping pupils to line up quietly outside the class
- photocopying
- sharpening pencils
- supplying spellings
- offering comfort in times of adversity (this includes to the teacher)
- monitoring the learning and behaviour of the class and individual pupils
- taking small groups in literacy, numeracy and other curriculum areas
- helping children use the computers
- accompanying the teacher to swimming lessons and school trips
- removing troublesome pupils from class
- helping pupils with learning difficulties
- carrying out literacy or numeracy intervention programmes
- carrying out social-skills or motor-skills intervention programmes
- preparing resources and materials for lessons, such as mixing paints or getting out PE equipment
- encouraging reluctant pupils to participate in lessons
- putting up displays
- taking down displays
- supervising at playtimes
- selling the school tuck.

Supporting the school

TAs are expected to work towards fostering the general ethos of the school. Extended schools, in which provision of care for children beyond the usual school day is offered, are becoming increasingly common. You may be employed to assist with running breakfast clubs or after-school homework or sports clubs. Starting off the school day with a healthy, filling meal and having somewhere quiet to complete homework may have a big impact on children's learning, and these opportunities are vital for many. In addition, TAs may assist in activities that take place off-site or out of school hours – such as school visits, residential trips, concerts, plays and parents' evenings.

Now that we have looked at what the TA job may involve, the next chapter will tell you how to go about getting a TA job and the qualifications you may need.

I don't like it when I am suddenly taken away from the child I am supporting to do photocopying, or some other task. I feel I am letting the child down.

I don't have to take home any work like the teachers. When I'm finished, I'm finished.

In this school, all of us TAs feel like second-class citizens – we are not invited to staff meetings or planning meetings and we have our own room to sit in. We don't mix with the teachers at all.

Chapter 2
Getting the job, getting on in the job

Going for the job

Schools usually start the search for a TA by placing an advert in the local newspaper as well as in the job sheets which individual LAs send out weekly to all their schools. Schools may also advertise jobs on their websites. Adverts often attract an enormous response. One head teacher recently advertised for a teacher to join his senior management team and had no response; in the same week he received 163 responses for a TA post. TA jobs are popular — particularly with women with families, as the school hours and holidays fit their lifestyle. It is a pity more men do not apply. Many of our pupils now live in single-parent families where there is an absent father. The presence of a male TA to act as a male role model would be a great asset to any school.

If you are thinking about applying, consider the following:

- Is this a job that really interests me?
- Are my personality and skills suited to such a job?
- Can I work the times required by the school?
- Does the advert ask for any qualifications? If so, do I have them or something equivalent?
- Am I willing to undertake training to achieve qualifications if that is part of the job specification?
- Is the pay adequate for my needs?
- Will I be able to cope with the demands of the job?

What the school is looking for

When schools are appointing a TA, an applicant's personal qualities, enthusiasm and willingness to learn will be considered alongside qualifications and experience. You will be working closely with pupils, teachers, parents and professionals from outside the school, so good interpersonal and communication skills are desirable. Reliability, a well-developed sense of humour and the ability to use your initiative are key attributes too.

When a school is considering your application, they will tend to look at whether you have:

- a relevant qualification, or the willingness to undertake one;
- previous experience with children;
- the ability to work as part of a team, and with both adults and children;
- skills and attributes suited to the job;
- a previous work record.

I like the way the job fits in with my own children. I can drop them off at their school and go straight to my own school. Then I can pick them up when they come out. It's perfect.

I like being part of a team. It makes me feel valued.

Be prepared

It will help to allay your fears before an interview if you feel prepared. If you don't know the school well, do some research on the Internet to find out more about it. In addition, before you even submit your application form or CV, you may ask the school if you may look around it and talk to a TA who works there about the role. The visit may kindle enthusiasm and provide knowledge that will be useful and can be reflected in an interview. On the other hand, you may decide after the visit not to pursue your job application.

You should also think about suitable questions to ask at the interview. Here are examples:

- What exactly will my role be?
- Will I have any training before I start?
- What training opportunities are available?
- What will my hours be?
- What is the pay?
- Will I get holiday or sick pay?
- Will my contract be temporary or permanent?

Some questions you may be asked

Taking some time to consider what questions you may be asked will also prove useful, and help you feel more confident. These are likely questions:

- What qualities do you think a good TA needs to have? How have you demonstrated these qualities yourself?
- What has your previous work experience been?
- Do you have any relevant qualifications?
- How would you go about creating a display?
- Would you be willing to volunteer to support the occasional out-of-hours school function?
- Are you computer literate?
- What would you do if a child in one of your groups refused to work?
- Have you ever worked with someone with SEN? What is your understanding of the term?
- What are your hobbies/interests?

The interview

When you arrive for your interview, you will almost certainly find yourself waiting with other short-listed candidates. It is unlikely that more than three or four candidates will be selected for interview, so remember that you have done well to get this far.

Interview panels vary, but will almost certainly include the head teacher and a school governor. The SENCo may attend if the role on offer includes any involvement with SEN pupils. Don't worry if you lack qualifications or training

I think we deserve more pay – we seem to have a lot of responsibility, it's an important job but the pay is poor.

as they will be looking at the whole person. They may choose you for the job even if you have no qualifications and others have. Alternatively, they may prefer someone with more experience with children than you – it all depends on the school's priorities. Just be yourself and answer the questions to the best of your ability, emphasising the positive and the skills you can bring to the job.

Food for thought

You can change your mind

Try to see the interview as a chance for you to interview them as much as the other way round. Ask yourself if you would feel happy working in this school, and with the people interviewing you. If you don't think you would, you can always say you don't think it's the right job for you after all. That is better than starting the job and giving up after a few weeks.

If at first you don't succeed, try, try again.

Not this time

If you don't get the first TA job you go for, don't be disillusioned. TA jobs are frequently advertised. The government is investing lots of money in raising standards and enabling pupils with SEN to access the curriculum effectively, and TAs play a big part in this. After an unsuccessful interview it would be useful to reflect on why another person got the job. You could even contact the school where you had your interview to ask for some pointers for your next interview. Maybe it would help if you worked voluntarily in a school to gain experience. Perhaps you could study for some kind of qualification. Bear in mind that if they liked you, the head is likely to keep your details on file and may contact you if another job comes up.

Success

Congratulations! A new phase in your life is about to begin, with opportunities to develop your knowledge and skills, to meet people from many different walks of life and to make a real difference in the lives of vulnerable children.

Anyone who works with children has to have a police check. The LA will organise this when the school informs them of your appointment. You will not be able to start your job until this is complete.

You will then be issued with your contract, be it temporary or permanent, and a job description that outlines exactly what your duties are. These duties will depend on whether you are employed as a general TA or to work more closely with one or more children with SEN, as well as your level of qualifications.

Job structure and qualifications

We can do various courses to get some qualifications, but it makes no difference to our pay and is a lot of hard work. Why should we bother?

For many years there were no set qualifications for TAs. One survey found they were presenting more than three hundred different qualifications, some more relevant than others. In addition, there was little incentive for TAs to seek any accreditation as there was no differentiation in the level of pay. This was reflected in the number of TAs who had no relevant qualifications. The National Occupational Standards (NOS) were introduced in 2001 in an effort to introduce some consistency, fairness and clarity to the role of TAs. This document is an

NOS framework:
www.tda.gov.uk/upload/
resources/pdf/t/ta_nos.pdf

www.tda.gov.uk/partners/
supportstafftraining/
framework

I need more training – I am not always sure if what I am doing is the best for the child.

important reference as it provides a framework to ensure best practice. The Training and Development Agency (TDA) have developed a career framework and guidance for support staff. Schools can use this framework to identify progression and training opportunities for TAs and other support staff.

National Vocational Qualifications

The DfES supported the introduction of the NOS and introduced National Vocational Qualifications (NVQs) for TAs in 2002. The role of a TA is now governed by a set of uniform standards that outline levels of responsibility and ensure these are linked to qualifications and pay. There are four NVQ levels.

Level 1: TAs working at level 1 will be involved with non-teaching aspects of the work: preparing resources, displaying work, photocopying and other time-consuming but essential activities. There will be little contact with children, but a police check will still be required. Qualities such as reliability, efficiency and the ability to show initiative would be sufficient to work at this level. No formal qualifications are required and this level obviously attracts the least pay. Some TAs are happy to continue providing this useful level of service and remain working at level 1 throughout their career.

Level 2: Most schools need TAs who are able to work at level 2, and most TAs begin working at this level. These TAs are involved much more in the teaching process, working closely alongside pupils and teachers. They help with classroom resources and records as well as supporting individuals and small groups of children. This may include assisting with literacy and numeracy activities in the classroom, supporting the use of ICT, and helping to manage pupils' behaviour. There may be pupils with SEN within the groups or classes they support, but their job at this level is usually to support across all levels of ability.

If a TA at this level has no relevant qualification, the school may encourage them to obtain an NVQ level 2, which may result in higher pay. There are some TAs who have been employed for some time who choose not to qualify, and remain working at this level.

Level 3: TAs working at level 3 usually have some previous experience of working in schools, and will generally be given more responsibility. Their work will require additional skills and knowledge. For example, they may be working with pupils with SEN, they may lead a team of TAs, or they may be the sole TA in a particular department, responsible for supporting all the teachers in it. The NVQ level 3 for TAs, or an equivalent, would normally be expected of those working at this level. You need not have a level-2 qualification before acquiring a level 3, provided you have a sufficient range of responsibility to complete the units of competence required.

A level-3 NVQ is also considered an appropriate grade for a cover supervisor role. These TAs are employed to supervise pupils while they carry out work that has been previously planned and prepared by the teacher. The Workforce

Agreement Monitoring Group (WAMG) guidance states that cover supervision should only be carried out for short-term absences.

Since September 2005, following the national agreement on remodelling the school workforce which was signed in 2003, teachers have been entitled to spend 10 per cent of their timetabled time out of the classroom, for carrying out planning, preparation and assessment (PPA time). Cover supervisors should not cover PPA time.

Level 4: TAs working at level 4 will have HLTA status, and can take on a more responsible role than a cover supervisor. The national agreement on remodelling introduced HLTA status to ensure adequate provision for the teaching of whole classes when teachers take their PPA time. On achieving HLTA status, a TA is able to teach classes previously planned in conjunction with the teacher, without the teacher being present. HLTA status opens up the possibility of taking on a wide variety of more responsible roles – some act as specialist assistants for a subject or department; some help develop support materials for pupils.

www.tda.gov.uk/support/hlta/ professsstandards

The HLTA standards identify what candidates need to demonstrate in order to be awarded HLTA status.

Do I need a TA qualification before I apply for a job?
It is not mandatory for TAs to have relevant qualifications. Indeed, to acquire level-2 or level-3 NVQ you will need to be in post; you need to provide evidence of real work situations in order to gain these. Schools will often indicate in a job advert that the successful candidate will be expected to undertake a relevant qualification if they don't already have one. It is up to the school and the LA to decide if any qualifications you have are adequate for the required level.

For contact details of LAs:
www.dfes.gov.uk/
localauthorities/
index.cfm?action=authority

How much will I be paid?
This will vary between schools and LAs. However, it is usual to consider the level of responsibility and qualifications of the TA.

Achieving HLTA status
Funding
If you wish to apply for HLTA status, you should approach your head teacher or line manager and ensure you have school support. HLTA training is funded by the TDA via your LA. There will be a named HLTA contact in your authority who will give you more information. To begin training, you will need to have two years' experience in school as well as qualifications in literacy and numeracy. If you don't have the necessary qualifications, your LA may fund training for you. The LA is required to publish details of their process for selecting candidates. The training is a continuous programme rather than a one-off course.

http://www.tda.gov.uk/
support/hlta/becomingahlta

Training for HLTA status

- *Assessment-only route*: For very experienced TAs who are already covering the thirty-one standards required in their daily work in school. These TAs will simply attend the three-day preparation course as outlined below.
- *Full training*: For less experienced TAs, who are not meeting all the standards during the course of their work. These TAs will be offered a full training programme before they will be able to attend the three preparation days.
- *Tailor-made programmes*: For people who do not need full training but are not ready for the assessment-only route. These TAs may need additional training in specific areas. It is normal to conduct an initial assessment of their needs; training will be based on these. Usually, around five additional training days will be required.

Preparation for assessment

Training will vary, but all candidates will undergo the same preparation and assessment process. This involves attending three preparation days at a centre organised by the LA, where candidates will get the chance to meet other TAs from their LA. The process will involve:

- understanding the professional standards and how they relate to your work in school;
- preparing for the four assessment tasks all candidates must complete;
- receiving formative feedback on the assessment tasks from your facilitator;
- preparing for the visit to your school by an assessor.

Candidates will be assigned a facilitator, who will explain the four tasks they will need to carry out in schools. These are designed to enable TAs to demonstate how they are meeting the professional standards in their work. They consist of the following:

- working with an individual pupil;
- working with a group;
- working with a whole class;
- describing five other situations or events they have encountered, usually out of the classroom, to ensure they meet all the standards.

The final task in the list will enable TAs to 'mop up' any standards they may not have been able to demonstrate in the three previous tasks.

After the course, each candidate is allocated an assessor (who will not be the same person as your facilitator) who will provide feedback on the assessment tasks and visit your school no later than twelve working weeks after your last preparation day.

Case study

Ann Smith, TA Stetchworth Heath School

I attended three days at my local centre since it was felt that my level of experience meant I needed no additional training, and I already had the maths and literacy qualifications I needed. I was the only person there from my school, but it was good to meet up with other TAs from other schools, and we all got along well. We were all in the same boat and were able to support each other.

On day 1 we were told all about the four tasks, and given response sheets in order to complete them. The facilitator was really helpful and by the end of the first day we knew just what was expected and how to go about the tasks. On day 2 we had to bring one of the tasks completed and two of the others in draft form. We were given an opportunity to discuss our work, which helped us to see for ourselves what else needed to be done. We had to make sure that the statements we had written on our response sheets met the relevant standards. For example, one of the standards is 'They know a range of strategies to establish a purposeful learning environment and to promote good behaviour.' I met this standard in my tasks by outlining a situation which happened in class:

One of the pupils shouted out the answer, so I reminded the whole class of the rule that before we answer a question we put our hands up.

On day 3 we had to take in the response sheets for the first three tasks and task-4 sheets in draft form. The facilitator gave us some general feedback on how we were getting on. By the end of the day, we knew when we had to send our completed task forms back, and what we had to do back in school to arrange for the assessment visit. We all swapped email addresses and decided to meet up at one of our houses to discuss how we were getting on at a later date.

Assessment

This involves a half-day visit from your assessor, who will cross-reference your collected evidence against the standards to ensure you have met them. The assessor will talk to the head teacher, to the teachers with whom you work most closely, and predominantly to you. They will already have seen your response sheets and will have some questions to ask on these. They will also want to see the documentary evidence supporting your tasks, which should be kept in a file. This evidence may include photocopies of planning sheets, reports or case studies, photographs of classroom resources, and examples of pupils' work.

After the assessment day, the assessor will send their recommendation to the regional provider of assessment for moderation. Moderation takes place regularly and you will normally receive your result within eight weeks. There are three possible outcomes:

1. All the standards have been met and you will receive a letter informing you of this.
2. Up to three standards have not been met and you are suitable for a partial reassessment. Arrangements for this will be discussed with you.
3. There is insufficient evidence that all the standards have been met and you will not be recommended for HLTA status.

At the time of writing, there are over eight thousand HLTAs in England, and at least 90 per cent of TAs who apply for the status are successful. Up to a further 8 per cent may need a partial reassessment, but then go on to achieve the status.

What are the benefits of HLTA status?

Two TAs share their views when part-way through the three-day HLTA course.

Sharoon Mawjee, TA Gatton School, Wandsworth
I heard about the HLTA programme from my head teacher and took it on because I wanted to extend my professional development. I saw it as a way of learning more about teaching, which I've always wanted to do, although I knew the teacher would be responsible for deciding what I taught and would also assist me with the planning.

As I didn't have Maths and English qualifications which were acceptable in the UK, before I could start the course I had to overcome my fear of maths and take my level-2 adult numeracy and literacy test at the local professional centre. I managed to get through – and that was the easy part!

When I came to the first day of the HLTA class I began to understand just how much work I had to put in. I knew it would be worth it. It would give me the opportunity to cover classes and gain a greater understanding of my work. I'm happy to have got this far and know it is only the first step in my desire to be a teacher.

Leigh Keefe, TA St Anselm's School, Wandsworth
I started working as a TA five years ago, in order to fit in with my children's school holidays. After working in an office for most of my career, it was a great change. The diversity of the children I found myself working with was astounding to me, and initially it was difficult to know if I was helping them to achieve as individuals. I knew that I wanted to learn more, so when my head teacher spoke to me about the HLTA course I thought it would be the ideal opportunity to gain further knowledge and understanding of my job. I knew it would be a challenge but I wanted to push myself that little bit more. I think if I acquire the status my confidence will grow, especially when it comes to communicating with parents and teachers. In addition, it will help me to know that I am contributing effectively to children's learning. It's also been interesting to realise how I am already meeting the HLTA professional standards through my current work. All I have to do in the tasks is prove it!

Is it worth the effort to obtain HLTA?

Case study

Mohammed Patel

When I achieved HLTA status, I was very pleased. When I undertook it, I knew there may not be an HLTA post available in school for me, and there isn't, but I learned so much it was worth it for that alone. Also, my self-esteem has risen. I am really proud of the fact that I was able to apply myself to all that work and succeed. I just wish I'd done that when I was in school!

I've now begun looking for another job with the status. I've noticed there are more and more HLTA jobs advertised, offering a higher salary, and it's great that I'm now in a position to apply for these jobs. I think it's definitely been worth the effort.

The truth is that opportunities for HLTAs are limited and schools are not always able (or willing) to finance the role. There was some resistance to the status originally as some felt it was 'teachers on the cheap', with non-teachers being used to fill a role that should be undertaken only by teachers. Just because you complete the HLTA course, it does not mean you will easily find an HLTA job or achieve a salary commensurate with the role. However, you will certainly further your knowledge about the job, feel more confident about your skills, and understand just what an important job you are able to do. The value of HLTAs within the education system is now being recognised, and as attitudes towards them change, more schools are gradually employing them.

Conclusion

The NFER's research into the deployment and impact of support staff who have achieved HLTA status reveals a largely positive picture. The HLTA role has clearly grown and developed since it was introduced in 2003. In line with its original purpose, HLTA status is offering recognition and valuable development opportunities to support staff as well as providing assistance to pupils, teachers and schools. It is clear that the HLTA role has the potential to change the way in which education is delivered and to make a positive difference to school life. It offers greater flexibility to school leaders as well as greater job satisfaction for staff.

NFER (2007)

The introduction of nationally agreed levels for TAs has led to more consistency in terms of job expectations, pay and conditions, which can only be of benefit to you as a TA. In the next chapters, we shall explore in more detail the type of support you may be expected to offer as a TA, and the strategies you may use.

Chapter 3
Supporting pupils

There is a destiny that makes us brothers: none goes his way alone. All that we send into the lives of others, comes back into our own.

Edwin Markham

"Ensure the reward relates to the child's preferences and age."

In your job as a TA, you will be expected to support children's learning in a number of ways. It is important to consider those aspects of a child's well-being that underpin effective learning before looking at the teaching and learning process itself. For example, children are unlikely to concentrate or progress well if they aren't motivated, if they feel so bad about themselves that they expect to fail, or if poor behaviour prevents them from staying on task. There is a lot you can to do to help in these areas. That is what this chapter focuses on.

Motivation

Children need encouragement, praise and rewards to motivate them. This applies particularly to pupils with learning difficulties: many become disillusioned and reluctant to work. They may feel embarrassed about the quality of their work in comparison to that of their classmates.

Action plan

- Find out how the school's reward system works. It may involve house points, stickers, marbles in a jar, certificates or other forms of acknowledgement. Ensure your reward system fits in with the school's.

- Have your own supply of stickers to give out for good effort or behaviour. You need something to hand out to acknowledge children's efforts.

- Many children enjoy being given jobs to do as a reward. These include giving out books, showing a visitor to the head teacher's office and returning the register. Children may regard being given simple tasks as rewards for all sorts of reasons; but the key one is that it shows you trust them to do something responsible.

- Ensure the reward relates to the child's preferences and age. Gav from Year 8 may not appreciate a teddy bear sticker saying 'Excellent work'. He might prefer five minutes on the computer at the end of a lesson.

- Verbal praise works well. Saying 'Well done' and smiling or nodding your head to acknowledge the effort a child is making get the message across and may help a child stay on task.

- Bear in mind that if children are praised for every little thing, they may become too reliant on praise. Use your discretion and try to praise appropriately and sincerely.

Some pupils with low self-esteem will doubt your sincerity, however genuine it is, owing to their lack of self-regard. Other techniques, incorporating a more subtle praise and reward system, are required for these.

- Make use of body language: a touch on the shoulder, a wink or a thumbs-up shows you've noticed the quality of, or effort put into, their work and may work wonders.

○ Show them you are on their side and that you like and value them. Stick up for them if someone is unfair or unkind. Smile at them as you pass them in the corridor.

○ Showing an interest in their lives and their work is important. Ask them if they enjoyed the football match they watched last night.

As your relationship with them grows and their self-esteem develops, you can move on to use the same praise and reward system as you use with other pupils. Your own self-esteem and sense of achievement will grow when you see that your unobtrusive intervention has been effective.

Case study

Paul was a 10-year-old pupil with a troubled family background who had already been excluded from three schools. Maia, his TA, did not know how to deal with him, but she realised that he was very unhappy. He often refused to work, would leave the classroom without permission, and would frequently fight with other children. When he had done something well, he hated being praised for it. On one occasion, when Maia had written 'Well done' on a piece of writing he had done and hung it on the wall, he scribbled all over it.

Gradually, Maia learned to give Paul recognition in a way he could accept. If she saw he had behaved or worked well, she would smile, wink or give a thumbs-up sign. When she could get him on his own, she would say how pleased she was with him. Paul responded well to this, and didn't seem to mind receiving praise in this less public way. At some level he knew she understood him and gradually he was able to accept praise in the same way as the other children did. It was as if he had not felt he had deserved it before, but once she had found a way that was acceptable to him, he was able to take on board her positive comments and begin to believe them.

Difficult behaviour

The behaviour of some children stops me from getting on with the work. I wish I did not have to have these children in my group.

The first thing to do is find out the school rules on behaviour, including the policy for dealing with bad behaviour and rewarding good behaviour. You will need to know what sanctions are available to you and how these are imposed if a child misbehaves. Pupils can be very devious, and may try to gain easy rewards by assuring you, for example, that they are always given a house point for completing a piece of work. You will feel much more confident about dealing with these situations if you are aware of the ground rules. Consistency is really important, so use the rules the pupils are used to and don't be taken in.

I do not get enough help with badly behaved children in my group. I think the teacher just likes to get rid of them onto me. I do not have enough experience to deal with uncooperative children.

It is vital to discuss with the class teacher what behaviour they expect from pupils. You can agree with the teacher a clear set of measures that you can impose should a pupil in your group misbehave. If a pupil continues to be difficult and the situation becomes intolerable, you should send that pupil back to the class and discuss the matter with the teacher after the lesson. This pupil should perhaps be removed from the group, but it may have been an isolated incident.

Action plan

○ Find out your role in giving out rewards and sanctions. What rewards can you provide? Are you able to keep pupils behind or recommend detention?

○ Be consistent: children respond best when they know exactly what the rules are and what to expect.

○ Ensure that any rewards or sanctions you impose are carried out. If you say pupils must miss five minutes of their morning break, that must happen. If not, pupils are unlikely to believe you next time you promise them a reward or sanction, and any treat or punishment will be less effective.

○ Judge the behaviour and not the child. After an incident has occurred, wipe the slate clean and try not to bear a grudge.

○ Concentrate on the positive. Congratulate the pupil who is working quietly, so they become a role model for the desired behaviour, while ignoring the child who is playing up, if possible. Say 'Well done, Salman, for getting on with your work and ignoring the noise around you. You deserve a house point' or 'See the way Claire is sitting quietly with her legs crossed and arms folded, looking at Miss Bridges. Can we all do that?'

○ Learn to replace 'please' with 'thank you'. 'Please will you work quietly?' could be considered a request and the response could be 'No'. If you say 'Work quietly. Thank you,' you are assuming your instructions will be followed, making a powerful statement that is more likely to be obeyed.

○ Find as many ways as you can to praise pupils. For example, you could thank them if they have behaved well or offer congratulations if they bring back their homework on time. This will increase self-esteem as well as helping them form a good relationship with you. If they like and respect you (and feel that you like and respect them) they are far less likely to misbehave.

I love it when I can see my SEN pupil has really improved – I feel proud of him.

Case study

Nazima, TA

Last week, when I was reading a book on animals with a group of pupils, two of them kept on making animal noises. This was disrupting the session and making the whole group laugh, except for two children. I congratulated the two boys for not joining in with the laughter, and for continuing to concentrate. Without naming any of the group, I said I was aware some pupils were finding it difficult to settle, but I felt they had had long enough now. I reminded them of the school rule not to shout out without putting their hands up. I said if anyone broke the rule from now on, then they would stay behind at playtime and read the book to me on their own. One boy continued to be silly, so I calmly told him that he would have to stay behind. He was very quiet after that, and when it came to playtime, he asked me if he could go out as he had been good since then. I was very tempted to give in, especially as I was dying for a cup of tea, but I knew I had to stick to my word, and I did. In the lesson today, his behaviour was fantastic, and I had my cup of tea at break time!

Independence

Your role as a TA is to support a pupil to enable them do their own work and be as independent as possible. By working independently, children experience a sense of achievement and begin to feel better about themselves; their self-esteem and behaviour often improve as they see themselves making progress. It is important not to allow children to become too attached and dependent upon you; that is a misdirection of the kindness and compassion that enables you to be a good TA. When your time working together comes to an end, if they have always had you there helping them all they will have learned is that they can't do things on their own.

I feel I have made a difference to many of the pupils I worked with. This is great job satisfaction. Much better than working as a secretary, which is what I did before.

Food for thought

John, I am very disappointed with your work.
Say how you feel, not how lazy he is. He will become very defensive if you criticise him.
You have only written two sentences. Look, last week you did really well and completed seven.
Identify the problem and show the evidence that he is capable of writing much more.
Will you explain to me why you have written so little this week? Thank you.
You are giving him a chance to express his point of view.
You're blaming Jack for talking to you so you couldn't concentrate. But you could have told me at any time that you weren't able to get on with your work. I don't think that's a reasonable excuse. I want you to finish this at home.
You have applied a sanction in a firm and fair way. You have not raised your voice or pointed the finger of blame. This will help maintain or improve your relationship with the child.

Action plan

How do you spell onomatopoeia?

How about we look that one up in a dictionary?

- ◗ Have high expectations of pupils you work with, no matter how complex their needs. Encourage them to strive to achieve more. Do not accept work into which they have put little effort.

- ◗ Encourage them to work independently by equipping them with study skills. For example, teach them how to use a dictionary instead of telling them how to spell a word. You could provide pupils with a list of key words they are likely to need in a lesson. Ask the teacher beforehand what these will be so you can prepare the list in advance.

- ◗ Rather than doing work for them, give them the tools to do the work themselves. This may involve giving them a writing frame so they have a clear structure for their own writing, or a number line to help with their sums.

- ◗ Discuss the strengths and weaknesses of their work with them. Awareness of their own learning goals will help them to feel involved and motivated. For example, 'You have worked hard on your handwriting today. It is looking much neater. Well done! Tomorrow we'll concentrate on getting the spacing between words more even.'

- ◗ Promote a have-a-go culture. Emphasise that it's often only by trying to do something and making a mistake that we learn how to do it better the next time.

- ◗ If a child is reluctant to play with others in the playground or to join in social situations, find out why and discuss strategies for dealing with what they are finding difficult. You could encourage other pupils to play with them or set up a social skills group.

You work with Donna, a statemented pupil, for ten hours a week. You see her struggle with her work. You know a bit about her family background and are aware that things are difficult. You get to know her and want to help her all you can. The skill is to do this whilst encouraging her self-reliance.

Donna feels secure with you. You encourage the relationship, letting her know that you value and accept her just as she is. You don't allow other pupils to bully her – you will deal with this if it occurs. You have high expectations of her, both in terms of her work and her behaviour. You teach her how to become an independent speller by showing her how to use a dictionary and giving her a wordbook in which to write down the words she finds difficult. You talk to her about what she enjoys, as well as what she finds difficult and the areas in which she would like to improve. You use this knowledge to inform your own discussions with the teacher and SENCo about her IEP targets.

Donna doesn't have many friends and asks to stay with you at lunch and break times. You talk to her about her concerns and role-play ways of initiating games and conversations. You assign her a playground buddy.

You understand that enabling Donna to deal with difficult situations is far more important than rescuing her from them. When she moves on, she will be an independent, confident child – thanks to you.

You give but little when you give of your possessions. It is when you give of yourself that you truly give.

Kahlil Gibran

Self-esteem

People with high self-esteem place value on themselves, believing they are worthwhile people. They are more likely to be happy and successful, and find it easier to make healthy and lasting relationships. People who have low self-esteem do not value themselves, and feel unworthy. Such beliefs can be self-perpetuating; as a result of their negative self-regard they tend to treat themselves and others badly, which creates negative scenarios confirming their low sense of self. Research has shown that adults with self-esteem issues are more likely to be involved in crime and in drug and alcohol abuse, and may develop mental illness or be involved in unsatisfying relationships.

As a TA you are in a powerful position to offer support in this area. Your job enables you to build close relationships with children, and you will frequently work in one-to-one situations and in small groups. Through the quality of the relationship you build with a child, their self-esteem may be raised.

Many pupils with SEN have low self-esteem. They know that their skills are less well developed than those of others. They will often identify themselves as 'thick'. Fellow pupils sometimes use such a word to describe them. Make it clear that this is not an acceptable term, and that you want everyone to do their best, rather than criticising the work or appearance of others. Pupils with SEN are often vulnerable and may need your support in standing up to bullying. Don't undervalue the impact of your relationship on such children.

Dennis Lawrence says in *Enhancing Self-esteem in the Classroom* (1996):

A vast body of evidence has accumulated showing a positive correlation between self-esteem and achievement, and with regard to self-esteem and school achievement in particular … There is clear evidence that relationships between teachers (and that includes TAs) and students can be either conducive to the enhancement of high self-esteem or conducive to reducing self-esteem.

There are lots of ways to help boost a child's self-esteem. Generally speaking, you need to build a close relationship with them in order to make them feel they are worth caring about and investing time and effort in:

- Show the child you value them. 'You have tried so hard today, I'm really proud of you.'
- Be on time for your lesson or session. If you are not going to be there, explain why to the children the previous day. 'I'm going on a training course tomorrow which is important to me. I'm sorry I won't be here. Of course I'll miss you, but I'll see you as usual the day after.'
- Have all your equipment ready and make sure the room in which you are working is as comfortable as you can make it.
- Make an effort to remember all the children's names and birthdays. 'I have written your names on these sticky labels. Would you mind wearing them until I have learned your names?'
- Say sorry if you make a mistake.
- Make sure that the work you are doing is appropriate for the pupil – not too easy or too difficult. If you feel there is a problem, discuss it with the teacher.
- Thank children for any job they have done or contribution they have made during the session.
- Do not allow pupils to abuse you or each other and never criticise the pupil, only the negative behaviour. 'Amil, I will not allow you to speak to other children in the group in that way. Aneka now feels upset because you called her an unkind name. What can you do to put it right?'
- Treat pupils equally and with respect at all times.
- Listen to what pupils want to tell you, without allowing this to impinge too much on the lesson. 'Hayley, I really want to hear about the dance competition. Could you tell me about it at the end of the lesson?' (It's amazing how the desire to tell you a long and detailed story disappears when playtime comes.)
- Remember to ask how a child's sick grandma is or how their dog got on at the vet's after his operation. If a child goes into hospital, send a card.
- When a child leaves an individual session with you, say goodbye and tell them that you look forward to the next session.
- Watch out for any sign of child abuse and report it immediately to the class or head teacher, or designated personnel. Any unusual marks on the child's body should be reported, especially if they look uncomfortable when you ask how the mark got there. Other clues may be observed in something a child writes or draws, or through unusual behaviour. It is important not to jump to

"I thought you wanted to tell me about your new pet!"

conclusions. You should not make any false promises to the child that you won't tell anybody if they do disclose anything to you; it is your duty to pass this information on. Your school should provide you with detailed child protection procedures; ensure that you are familiar with these.

Case study

Lorna started working with Hamish when he was 12. He was a 'looked after' child, who had been rejected by his alcoholic mother when he was 8, and who had no idea who his father was. He had a red birthmark on his face and was overweight. Hamish was often bullied and would respond by becoming very angry and upset. He began to have a lot of time off school.

Lorna had been assigned to work with him for three hours a week owing to his learning difficulty. She arranged to see him twice a day for ten minutes. He learned to trust her and told her any concerns he had at their meeting at the beginning of the day. At the end of the day, they met to discuss how he had got on. If things had gone wrong they would talk about why and what could be done to prevent it happening again. He had permission to seek Lorna out during the day if he really needed to.

The fact that he felt someone cared about him had a powerful effect. It took a long time, but he became more confident and less concerned about the mark on his face. He began to make friends and then, with Lorna's support, he lost 2 kilos in weight. Hamish is now studying for his GCSEs and is expected to do well. Lorna knows she made a difference to his life, and that made her realise just how important a TA's role can be.

This integrated approach ensures the child is ready to learn. We shall now look at ways of supporting the learning process itself.

Chapter 4
Supporting learning

Support across the curriculum

A large part of a TA's job will be support of children's learning. If you work in a primary school this will often be in literacy and numeracy lessons, although you may be working with children across the curriculum in subjects such as science, ICT, history and geography. The type of support you provide will vary depending on the age range and ability of the pupils as well as the subjects. This chapter will provide you with tips on how to support children in the classroom generally. It will also give you basic information about such key areas of learning as reading, writing and numeracy, and advice for helping in these areas.

Before you start, be prepared. Have ready all the equipment you may need:

- ◗ Pupils' books.
- ◗ Resources. (These should ideally be stored centrally. Prior to every lesson, get the resources you need and always replace them when you have finished with them.)
- ◗ Pencils, pencil sharpeners and rubbers. (Make sure that you get back what you give out. The same applies to games you play. Ensure every card is collected since missing items render games useless – then pupils get bored, which may lead to behavioural problems.)
- ◗ Stickers and certificates, or whatever the school uses to reward the pupils.

The Primary and Secondary versions of the DfES's Teaching Assistants File (both 2003) are designed to be used as initial training for TAs, and offer some good ideas for supporting pupils. They suggest that TAs can aid pupils' learning in the following ways:

- ◗ Drawing in reticent pupils who are too timid to put their hands up. Once you are aware of these pupils, you can give them encouragement, either by a nod or whispering something reassuring:'Go on, Reece, you know the answer to this.'
- ◗ Intervening on the pupil's behalf. This encourages them to participate in discussions and ensures they are given an opportunity to answer when they feel confident of their response: 'Mrs Crewdson, Charlie knows the answer to this.'
- ◗ Getting the ball rolling when pupils are slow to start a discussion: 'Leena, tell everyone about the animal we saw the other day in the book about zoos, and the sort of food he liked to eat.'
- ◗ Supporting less able or less confident pupils. These pupils need unobtrusive nodding, smiling, winking and eye contact. You may want to sit next to them during lessons to offer encouragement and ensure they have understood: 'Did you understand what Mr Kupczk just said? If not, I'll explain later.'

Sometimes I feel the teacher doesn't know what to do with me and I just sit there wasting my time.

www.teachernet.gov.uk/ publications

- Joining in and making your own contributions to class discussions: 'Well, I thought it was a really good book. I didn't like the ending, though, because…'.

I enjoy sitting in on lessons and watching the teacher. I have learned a lot myself!

- Demonstrating for the teacher. This may include telling them how you worked out a spelling, how you found a word in the dictionary or explaining some other way in which you found an answer to their question.

- Acting as devil's advocate. You could ask the teacher to explain something more fully (on behalf of a pupil whom you think may need more information).

- Echoing the teacher by repeating or rewording the phrase for pupils who may need help: 'Look, Hannah, Mr Byrne is showing you where the speech marks are. We know about those, don't we?'

- Acting as an extra pair of eyes. Observing the class and noticing which pupils clearly don't understand, which are not listening and at what point in the lesson the problem arose.

- Assisting with behaviour management. You can sit by a pupil who finds it hard to stay on task and is likely to be disruptive. At times you may need to take them out of the class and carry on working with them elsewhere – this is why it is important that you are involved with class planning.

- Resource management. This will include preparing, distributing and collecting pupil resources, and helping them use the resources.

www.qca.org.uk/qca_5101.aspx

The Qualifications and Curriculum Authority (QCA) have published suggestions about the contribution additional adults such as TAs working in classrooms can make. These include:

- integrating new pupils into school and classroom routines;
- boosting pupils' speaking and listening skills by engaging them in conversation whenever you get the chance;
- supporting pupils in maintaining concentration and participation;
- explaining and reinforcing lesson objectives;
- preparing individual pupils for lessons by, for example, reading the relevant chapter in advance of a lesson;
- making a note of pupils who are not coping with an exercise, so that the teacher knows which pupils will need to have that learning objective taught again at a later date to consolidate their learning of a particular concept or skill;
- valuing pupils' home languages and encouraging them to use them in their learning;
- supporting pupils to work collaboratively with their peers;
- helping pupils contribute to class discussions;
- monitoring progress and reporting back to teachers on successes and difficulties;
- reading and discussing texts with individuals or small groups to complement the guided and supported reading in the literacy hour in primary schools;
- acting as a scribe to record ideas.

She's always trying to get me to chat … perhaps she's a bit lonely!

"Boost pupils' speaking and listening skills by engaging them in conversation whenever you get the chance."

Literacy

Reading, writing and spelling are core skills. Pupils who fail to develop these skills adequately are at a great disadvantage as they underpin learning throughout the curriculum.

The National Literacy Strategy (NLS) was introduced into schools in 1998, and advocated a daily literacy hour. It was designed to make the teaching of literacy more consistent and to raise standards. In 2006 the Primary Framework for Literacy was introduced. It suggested a more flexible approach to the literacy hour, with more emphasis on speaking and listening.

**www.standards.dfes.gov.uk/
primaryframeworks/literacy**

Additional programmes to support literacy teaching have also been developed. TAs are often responsible for delivering these programmes, after receiving the necessary training:

- Early Literacy Support (ELS) – for children in Year 1 who are not making the expected progress;
- Year 3 Literacy Support – to accelerate the progress of children who need extra support beyond the usual literacy lessons;
- Further Literacy Support (FLS) – for children in Year 5, to help them achieve an age-appropriate level by the time they leave primary school.

Supporting reading

You will inevitably support pupils' reading skills. This may mean working with specific pupils with difficulties or hearing all pupils read. You will work under the direction of the teacher or SENCo. As you may realise, there is a lot more to hearing pupils read than just sitting listening. In order to help them progress as best they can, you should take an active approach.

Before you start, make sure the book you are using is at an appropriate level. Younger readers will be reading books that challenge them and there will be words they do not understand. If they are unable to read more than two words in every ten, they will need a different book to prevent frustration and a sense of failure.

Less able readers and younger readers need to be taught reading strategies. The four main ones are outlined below.

Picture cues

When learning to read we all took cues from pictures. For example, we were able to recognise the round red thing in the book as a ball. When we saw a picture of a ball with the word 'ball' underneath, we began to get the idea that the object was represented by a word.

With struggling or early readers, the information offered by the picture is important. If there is a picture on the page, discuss it with the child before they read the text and make sure they verbalise the words from the picture.

Talking about the picture helps them gain an understanding of what the text is about.

Never assume pupils know the names of things. Poor vocabulary may be a reflection of home circumstances in which there is little conversation or looking at books and few stimulating trips out, or it may indicate a difficulty the pupil has with making sense of language. Either way, it is important that vocabulary is discussed.

Sight vocabulary

Gradually, from around 18 months, children recognise and name various objects – Mummy, Daddy, Nan, pen, book, and so on. At around 3 to 4 years, many children start to recognise words as well as objects, and begin to read.

Children begin to acquire a sight vocabulary (words they can read) from their reading books ('Look, Mummy, that says cat!'), the television or computer, and through going shopping. Often the first word recognised and read is the child's own name. In nursery and reception classes teachers often label objects in the room – door, wall, floor, and so on – to encourage reading.

Letters and Sounds: Principles and Practice of High Quality Phonics (DfES, 2007) lists the 100 high-frequency words that recur most often in much of the written material young children read and that they need when they write. It also specifies at what phase these words should be learned, as well as providing tips on how they can be taught. It is well worth familiarising yourself with these lists as you may be involved in helping children to practise and learn these words. In addition to the words in this list, pupils will need to learn the key words from whatever reading scheme is used in the school.

To download *Letters and Sounds*, go to: www.teachernet.gov.uk/ publications

Context cues

Pupils bring their knowledge of the world to reading. Take the example of Laura-Jane, aged 5, who has been round the world twice, is taken out every weekend on stimulating visits and whose parents read to her every night. Her parents explain everything and value and ask for her opinion. Consequently, not only does she bring her extensive vocabulary and understanding to reading, she also brings confidence.

If Laura-Jane meets the sentence 'The boy went to the museum and saw a d…', she is able to guess the word 'dinosaur'. She's been to a museum, seen a dinosaur skeleton and would be confident enough to try her luck. Because she can understand what she is reading, she can self-correct. She can also predict what may happen next in the story.

Ryan, however, has seldom been past the end of his street, is part of a huge and dysfunctional family, has never seen the sea or been near a zoo or a museum, and lives in a house with no books and in which he is rarely spoken to. He will bring that experience to reading. He is quite likely to say something like 'The boy went to the museum and saw a deep.' He has a lack of understanding of the text so he is not able to use context cues to support his reading.

This is where the picture, if there is one, can come in handy. Ryan needs to see what a dinosaur looks like and be told what a museum is in order to build up his knowledge and understanding of the world. You can see the value of well-chosen school trips for children with Ryan's lack of experience. There is nothing like exposing children to reality to engage their attention and help them to learn.

Ryan's incorrect use of grammar may also put him at a disadvantage. If he is used to saying, for example, 'They was naughty children', he will struggle when he attempts to read grammatically correct sentences. It's more difficult for pupils who come to school when their life so far has not prepared them well for the world of reading. It is part of the TA's job to try to make up for some of this deficit and enable them to access the full curriculum as well as the joys of reading.

Phonics

When pupils encounter words that are not in their sight vocabulary, they need to be able to break them down into separate syllables like Man-ches-ter, or sounds like d-o-g. This strategy makes use of their phonic knowledge. Phonics is the skill of linking letter sounds (phonemes) to letters (graphemes). The greater their phonic knowledge, the more likely the pupil is to be able to build up the word. We need to teach pupils that words are made up of letters and that the letters, or combinations of letters, are represented by sounds.

From September 2006 all schools have been directed to use a synthetic phonics approach. This follows the publication in December 2005 of the Rose Review, which advocated this approach to reading. Synthetic phonics have been around for some time but have tended to be used as an intervention programme for pupils experiencing difficulties. This method teaches the forty-four sounds of letters or groups of letters within the English language initially, and then combines these sounds to form words. Analytic phonics is another method that has been taught in schools, often alongside synthetic phonics. In this approach, children are taught whole words and later analyse their constituent parts. *Letters and Sounds: Principles and Practice of High Quality Phonics* (2007) provides further guidance on the teaching of phonics and should be available in your school.

Underpinning an understanding of phonics is phonemic awareness. Pupils with poor phonological awareness will inevitably have problems learning phonics. It is likely therefore that as a TA you will assist some pupils on programmes to develop phonological awareness as well as phonics. Pupils need to be able to:

- listen;
- tap out or clap to a rhythm;
- recognise words that rhyme;
- recognise the onset and rime of a word – for example, in the word hug, h is the onset and ug is the rime;
- break words down into syllables – Liv-er-pool, play-time;

○ segment words into phonemes – shop is s-h-o-p;

○ blend phonemes into words – ch-a-t is chat.

It was great when my pupil read his first book – it made me feel great as well as him!

To be effective in supporting pupils' reading, you should encourage them to use all of these strategies. An older pupil may be struggling with reading because they didn't develop phonological awareness skills at the expected age, so you may be required to do work on blending and segmenting words with children in upper Key Stage 1 or Key Stage 2.

Food for thought
Listening to Fayed reading his book

Hello, Fayed. Nice to see you.

Let's look at your book. This looks interesting. What is the title? What do you think it is going to be about?

Let's look at the first page. Here is a picture. Tell me what you see. Who are these people? What are they doing? Do you see the ice cream in the picture – do you like ice cream? What do you think will happen next? Are there any questions you want to ask me about this page?

It is a good idea for you to read the text first, modelling how to read as you go by following the words with your finger. At the end of each page, ask Fayed to retell what has happened and then ask him to predict what may happen on the next page.

When Fayed reads, he may need to point to each word as he reads. When he gets stuck on a word, encourage him to use the most appropriate strategy to discover it. Do you need to ask him to refer to the picture or guess what the word is from the text? Is it a word he can build up using his phonological skills? It may be useful to repeat the sentence to give him support in guessing the correct word.

Skilled listening to readers enables you to find out areas of weakness:
• You may notice that they are unable to sound out words. They will need further phonic assessment and additional work in this area.
• They may show little understanding of the story they are reading. It would be important to offer further comprehension practice.
• You may notice they are not using the pictures for clues. You can show them pictures and talk together about what is happening in a picture and what its salient features are.

Supporting spelling
Spelling test

1. bote
2. scool
3. frend
4. wos
5. wen
6. bac
7. sed
8. shel

If only spelling were this simple! Spelling is an important skill, which can have a great impact on a pupil's confidence. Problems with spelling inhibit the creative flow of writing, and poor spellers will often use simple words they can spell rather than more complex words they would like to use. Poor spellers frequently make reluctant writers.

Knowledge of phonics is an important element in learning to spell, but not all words can be spelled using this method. For example, the word 'because', like many other words in the English language, cannot be worked out simply by using phonic knowledge.

Often pupils who are poor spellers rely too much on phonics for their spelling. Take this passage written by Ben, aged 10.

> won day I went to se my nan and she asked me wy
> I wos not at school I sed I wontid to play futball but
> I did not hav the rite kit sow I ad to go hom she giv
> me a choclat I luv me nan she sed wot a gud boy I am
> wen I say tankyu

Ben is confused and needs practice to build up his limited spelling skills. He should continue to work on his phonic knowledge, which is clearly limited, even though it is the method he is relying on to work out spellings. In addition, he needs to become aware of word patterns using onset and rime so that he can recognise the shape of words. The 'Look, Say, Cover, Write, Check' method would be most useful here. This requires the child to look at the word, say it, cover up the word, write the word and finally check to see if it is correct.

If spellings are practised in this way, using sets of words from the same word families as shown in the examples below, that helps to develop onset and rime skills.

ad	d-ad	ight	fl-ight
h-ad	gl-ad	n-ight	r-ight
s-ad	cl-ad	t-ight	l-ight

Rhythm – rhythm helps your two hips move

When two vowels go walking, the first does the talking – for words like 'oat' and 'eat'

Desserts or deserts – the sweet one has two sugars

Some words stand alone: they don't fit into any common spelling pattern, and can't be taught in this way. One method for dealing with these is to use mnemonics (memory aids) which provide ways to help the child remember how to spell a word. For example, 'because' could be remembered using the sentence 'Big elephants can't always use small exits.' There are many possible spelling aids, such as remembering 'necessary' with the mnemonic 'one collar, two sleeves'. Pupils should be encouraged to devise their own mnemonics and to illustrate them with a picture.

We need to help pupils to become independent spellers by teaching them strategies and by providing support to enable them to look for words themselves. Older pupils should be taught how to use a dictionary; younger and struggling pupils should keep a personal dictionary. They can write down unknown words to build up their own personal word bank.

In primary schools high frequency word lists are usually displayed on the classroom wall or provided as individual word lists. It is useful to prepare lists for specific topics. For example, if the science lesson is to be on the subject of flowers, prepare a list that includes petals, stamens, leaves, pollen and so on. Teaching children how to use the computer spell-checker is also useful, but beware. The computer cannot distinguish between alternative spellings.

Useful ways to teach spellings

I brushed my hare.
I eight my breakfast.
I picked up the male.

Is it right, Miss?
I spell-checked it on the computer.

- Give pupils plastic letters and ask them to spell words with them.
- Trace words in the air or use a sand tray to draw the words.
- Ask pupils to scan texts to find word families. For example, 'Highlight all the words you find that end in -ight, then after five minutes make a list and we shall see who has found the most.'
- Provide pupils with 'My spelling book' with twenty-six pages and a different letter at the top of each page, from A to Z. They use this to build up their own word bank.
- For early spellers, provide 'My picture spelling book' with twenty-six pages, and a letter from A to Z at the top of each. Give the child pictures of items beginning with each letter to stick on the relevant page. They should write the corresponding words underneath.
- When a pupil asks you for a spelling, tell them how to spell it but get them to write the word themselves in their books. Writing it correctly is the first step to spelling it.

Supporting writing

The development of writing skills may be affected by a pupil's spelling, handwriting, phonics, spoken vocabulary and knowledge of grammar. For pupils for whom English is an additional language, limited spoken and written vocabulary is an additional factor.

Before pupils are able to write, they need to have developed both hand–eye coordination and fine motor skills. Hand–eye coordination is the ability of the eyes to use the information received from the brain to direct and guide the hands to accomplish a given task. Fine motor skills enable the child to hold a pencil and write, and involve the refined use of the small muscles of the hand, fingers and thumb.

If you are working with very young children, or children who are struggling with this, you will probably be involved in providing activities that help them to develop these essential skills, such as drawing, painting, threading beads, cutting and sticking, making models with clay and Plasticine, and so on.

Many of the activities that parents may consider to be play are vital forerunners to the development of handwriting. How ready a child is to write will depend on what opportunities they have had to develop these skills before they attend school. The teacher will need to assess their needs and provide appropriate work. Some will be ready to write. Others will need programmes of work to develop hand–eye coordination and fine motor skills.

When pupils have reached the stage where they are able to write, they usually begin by copying words, often underneath a word written into their book. Their own name is a good starting point as they can recognise that and know what they are writing. As their skills develop, they will be able to put words together to make a whole sentence.

The best way to help struggling pupils is to identify the specific underlying problem as accurately as possible. Is the child able to use capital letters correctly? Is their letter formation holding them back? Is an inability to spell preventing them from writing more? Additional resources may be needed to support the area of weakness identified by the teacher and you; the class teacher will be able to provide the relevant resources.

Action plan

- Before pupils write anything, get them to say the sentence out loud. This helps them to form what they are going to say in advance, and see if it sounds right.
- Writing a daily diary, even with just one sentence, is good writing practice.
- Ensure pupils begin each sentence with a capital letter and end with a full stop.
- Once this has been achieved, you can go on to teach short-story writing, always encouraging the child to talk through the story before they write it down.

You will soon realise where the problems lie. Take this piece of work, for example, from Lee, a pupil in Year 7:

> My family
> one day me dad went to get me a bag of cips from the sop but he dropt the bag and it bost and the dog likt the chip and it wos not fer and I ad no tea

This writing reflects a range of problems: limited spoken vocabulary; poor spelling and phonic knowledge; lack of grammatical awareness; underdeveloped sequencing and sentence construction skills.

In this example, you would need to start by teaching the child how to produce a single independent sentence, bearing in mind that if their spoken vocabulary is limited you can't expect a high standard of writing. If Lee is unable to speak in whole sentences, he is unlikely to be able to write in them. You could work with him to produce one simple sentence in standard English, discussing aspects of spelling and grammar as you go: 'My dad got me a bag of chips from the shop.' He could use this sentence as a model for future reference.

It is also important for Lee to listen to the rest of his class, who can model language for him. Exposure to rich language is very helpful and is the best way for him to learn.

Supporting numeracy

If you work as a TA in a primary school, you will almost certainly be involved in supporting pupils' work in numeracy sessions. The National Numeracy Strategy (NNS) was launched in 1998 and implemented in primary schools from September 1999. The NNS standardised the learning objectives for children and advocated a three-part lesson for numeracy teaching: a 10-minute oral and mental starter to get the brain warmed up, a main teaching activity lasting 30–40 minutes, and then a 10-minute plenary clarifying and consolidating what has been learned.

www.standards.dfes.gov.uk/
primaryframeworks/
mathematics

The 'head-banging' part, going over certain points over and over again, can be very trying, thinking someone has 'got it' and then finding next day you have to start all over again.

The Primary Framework for Mathematics was renewed in 2006. This guidance encouraged greater flexibility in the structure of mathematics lessons, and contained less detailed objectives for the newly organised seven strands of learning. You will find it helpful to have your own copy of it, or at least be familiar with the numeracy objectives for the year groups with which you are working. You should be provided with the numeracy plans for the class, as well as developing an awareness of the types of resources you may be using and how they work.

For a pupil struggling with a mathematical concept, additional support and extra practice with a patient TA can have a big impact on their confidence.

When working with pupils in numeracy sessions, your role includes the following:

- Ensure all instructions have been interpreted correctly. Pupils need to know what is required of them, or they won't even begin working along the right lines.
- Work through examples with the children, reiterating the teaching point made earlier in the lesson.
- Look out for any difficulties or repeated mistakes that children are making, so you can feed this information back to the teacher.
- Ask the child how they arrived at a particular answer. Sometimes by finding out about their thought processes, you can see where they are going wrong and are in a better position to help them.
- Translate key vocabulary or phrases. Your teacher should have a copy of the DfES's Mathematical Vocabulary, which lists the key vocabulary for each year group. For example: 'We're working on capacity this week. That means we will be measuring liquids. I'll explain it all to you, but I think you'll find you know a lot about it already.'
- Show children how to use practical resources such as number lines or 100 squares, or other visual aids. 'Here is a number line. Shall we remind ourselves how to use it? For 8 add 5, start at 8 on the number line and count on 5 places. What's the number you're pointing to? 13. Well done. Now you can do the rest of the sums on your own.'
- Use ICT resources and suitable software, either with a group or with individuals as shown on their IEP.

I have learned to work computers. I had never been near a computer until I got this job.

Supporting other curriculum areas

You may find yourself helping pupils in other curriculum areas. TAs are increasingly used to support ICT and assist children with computer software to enhance their learning in a range of subjects. You should be given an opportunity to familiarise yourself with the relevant programs before using them with pupils. As regards other subjects, the more information you have in advance on the topics you will be working on, the more focused your support will be. The teacher you are working with should be able to provide you with half-termly or weekly subject plans. They should also give you clear guidance on how to work most effectively with your allocated pupil(s).

As well as being given specific activities to undertake with pupils, the type of general support you may give in these sessions may include:

- clarifying the task set by the teacher;
- assisting with spellings;
- discussing with the pupil how they should start or structure a writing task;
- encouraging the pupil to stay on task;
- setting time limits to complete a task;
- accompanying the pupil to the library to obtain relevant information or use the Internet to download suitable materials.

I liked it when the teacher introduced me to the class for the first time in a respectful way. Mrs Jones said, 'I want to introduce Miss Day. We are very lucky to have her. She is going to help us with our work. We would all like to welcome you here.' Even now, whenever I'm working with the class she will say something like 'It's our lucky day today. Look! Miss Day is here.' She is always clear about what she wants me to do, and then never forgets to thank me afterwards.

Whatever your role in the class, and however the teacher chooses to use your skills in the support of learning, it is your attitude towards the child – even more than the knowledge you bring to the lesson – that is most significant. A warm, sympathetic, interested and interesting TA is far more likely to enhance a pupil's ability to learn than a TA who is very knowledgeable about facts but not so good at communicating. The simple truth is, if pupils – particularly pupils in Key Stages 1 and 2 – like the person you are, they are more likely to produce their best work.

Chapter 5
Working with pupils with special needs

The success of the government drive to include the great majority of pupils with SEN in mainstream schools is largely dependent on the presence of well-trained TAs supporting teachers and pupils effectively. They may help to prevent some pupils developing learning difficulties in the first place.

Pupils in need of extra support will have been identified by the school as having a special need. Some TAs will be specifically employed to help such pupils, but those whose role is that of general classroom support will also encounter pupils with SEN. The opportunities TAs have to work closely with pupils mean that it is sometimes they who initially recognise the need of a pupil. As a TA, you have a responsibly to mention any concerns to the teacher.

Case study

I work with a group of low-ability pupils in Year 7 on a literacy scheme for low achievers. One of the pupils had great difficulty with reading and spelling, but he had really good general knowledge as well as a wide vocabulary. I went on a special needs course for TAs which outlined what the signs of dyslexia were. I reported my feelings to the class teacher, who passed my concerns on to the SENCo. He was diagnosed with dyslexia and started a different scheme more suited to his needs, which another TA had been trained to deliver. He is making better progress and is much happier. I am so glad I said something. It had not been picked up before as he had been to a lot of schools because his parents moved around a lot.

What do we mean by special needs?

The 2002 edition of the Code of Practice states:

A child has special educational needs if they have a learning difficulty which calls for special educational provision to be made for them.

A child has a learning difficulty if they have significantly greater difficulty in learning than the majority of children of their age, or if they have a disability that hinders them in making use of the usual educational facilities in their LA for children of their age. Special educational provision is additional to or different from the standard provision in schools (other than special schools). Bear in mind that although pupils with EAL may need additional support to access the curriculum, they should not be considered as having SEN unless it emerges that they are having problems with language acquisition which suggests they have a learning difficulty.

I feel inadequate sometimes when a child is struggling and I do not know what to do.

What does this mean for schools?

Some pupils already identified as having an SEN will come into school; for example, those born with severe physical, learning or sensory (visual or auditory) problems. If a school is aware that a child has SEN before they start school, provision can be made in advance. We cannot assume, however, that all pupils will be able to benefit from mainstream schools, despite the government drive towards inclusion. There will always be some children with such severe difficulties that they require a specially adapted education. It is the LA's responsibility to ensure such provision is available – usually within special schools or units attached to a mainstream school.

Most special needs are identified after a pupil starts school. Learning difficulties become apparent if the pupil is unable to meet the demands of the curriculum and does not progress with reading, writing or spelling at the same rate as their peers. More complex needs – such as dyslexia, dyspraxia or autistic spectrum disorders – may also become obvious after entry to school. Professional involvement is usually needed to ensure correct diagnosis and appropriate intervention.

When it first becomes obvious that a pupil is failing to make the progress expected or is displaying symptoms of a particular need, the class teacher will usually refer them to the SENCo. The concern will usually be registered in the first place by completing a record of concern or similar pro forma. This means the pupil's difficulties have been identified and their progress is being monitored. A TA may be responsible for this. The need may only be temporary: the child may cease to cause concern. If the problems persist, the school will take more formal action, according to the SEN Code of Practice. This sets out a framework for how schools should provide for their SEN pupils.

School Action

Once a child has been identified as having special needs, there will be further consultation between the teacher, SENCo and parents. The child is considered to be on School Action, which means that their needs can be met within the school, through an IEP. An IEP has four or five learning and/or behaviour targets that are relevant to the pupil's needs. The pupil's work is monitored and parents are encouraged to work with the child at home. The IEP is reviewed at least twice a year, and parents are invited to attend these reviews. As a TA you may be asked to give your feedback on the child's progress to inform the IEP writing. If the pupil fails to make progress at School Action, the school will apply to the LA to move on to School Action Plus.

I would like to have more say in what I do with the child instead of being told all the time what I must do.

School Action Plus

If the LA decides this is appropriate, a visiting professional will offer advice to the school regarding the targets on the IEP, and will usually monitor the pupil's progress, as well as providing training for the teacher or TA if a particular programme of work needs to be followed. Various outside professionals may become involved, depending on the child's needs. These may be drawn from the following:

- Educational Psychology Service
- Learning Support Service
- Behaviour Support Service
- Hearing Impaired Service
- Visual Impaired Service
- Speech and Language Therapy Service
- Pre-School Service
- Hospital Teaching Service

- clinical psychologists
- child psychiatrists
- paediatricians
- personnel from the health authority and social services
- Education Welfare Officer
- occupational therapists
- physiotherapists.

If a pupil makes good progress with the additional support, they may be moved back to School Action and, hopefully, in time not require any additional support. However, if the pupil fails to make adequate progress the school, with the permission of the parents, will apply to the LA for a statutory assessment to be made of the needs. As a result, the LA may decide to provide the pupil with a statement.

Pupils with statements

I work with a statemented pupil in science and the teacher does not provide any work for him to do that he can understand. It is all over his head and he gets very frustrated and so do I. I have told the teacher about the problem but he does nothing.

These pupils have been recognised by the LA as needing extra support in order to benefit from mainstream education. A statement is a document which declares the intention of the LA to provide financial aid to the school so they can employ a TA (or, if appropriate, a teacher or LA professional), as well as special equipment if required, in order that a child may continue in a mainstream school.

Early intervention

At School Action Plus some LAs provide financial support, which is often used to employ a TA on a short-term contract to support the pupil. This is becoming customary as it is of benefit to the pupil to receive support promptly rather than waiting for the protection of a statement. It helps the teacher, who may be finding it difficult to cope single-handedly with a particular pupil's difficulties. Parents also find early intervention reassuring. It may benefit the LA financially as it may reduce the likelihood of a child needing a statement later on.

Most pupils who receive this support make sufficient progress and do not go on to need a statement. However, there will always be children with a difficulty or disability who, without the security of regular support and access to ongoing professional advice, would not be able to stay in school. For these reasons schools, with the agreement of the parents, may make a request to the LA to make a statutory assessment.

IEPs

The IEP is a key document. IEP targets should be SMART (specific, measurable, achievable, realistic, time-targeted). It should be clear who does what, when and how. The IEP is central to the success of the SEN process. It is through the targets on it that we can focus on a pupil's needs and set up review meetings, enabling us to check the pupil's progress (or lack of it).

The quality of the IEP is important but, of course, it won't be worth the paper it is written on if the school fails to provide the circumstances and resources necessary to deliver it. If you find yourself lacking these, ask for something to be done since this will affect the quality of your work.

I would like to be involved when they are doing the IEP for the pupil I work with.

Usually the teacher and SENCo will devise the first IEP, having discussed the child's needs with the parents. The IEP follows careful assessments of the pupil, and the targets are based on the pupil's individual needs. The parents' agreed contribution is often written into the IEP. Once you begin working with the child towards achieving the targets, your views for any follow-up IEPs should be considered.

Each school will have its own preferred format for IEPs, and you should be talked through these by the SENCo or teacher. On the next page you can see an example.

Keeping SEN records

Many TAs find they are working with several pupils, groups and classes throughout the week. You should be given a timetable of where you should be, when, and with which class or pupil. The class teacher and SENCo will have copies of your timetable so that you can always be located easily. Checking the hours on your timetable is an efficient way of ensuring that pupils with statements are being allocated their recommended amount of TA time.

I have no time to record what has happened in the lesson.

Part of your responsibility as a TA will be to keep accurate and informative records for the pupils who have IEPs. There are several benefits to this:

◉ For your own information and as a reminder about what difficulties you observe in one session, so that you can plan effectively for your next session.

◉ For the class teacher, who needs to be kept up to date about what is happening. This information should be used in planning for the pupil.

◉ For the SENCo, who will need to monitor what you are doing and how the pupil is progressing.

◉ To provide you with information to prepare reports for review meetings.

◉ To observe particular patterns of behaviour or learning difficulties. You may see that Billy forgets his glasses for three out of five sessions with you, or Heather complains of headaches every time there is a reading session. Behaviour may be an important indicator of an underlying problem.

On pages 45–47 you will find examples of a completed IEP and a TA's record of work with a pupil who has an IEP, and also a blank template for the TA's record.

It's not my fault I lost them! I keep asking Mum for a new pair.

Billy, this is the fourth time you've forgotten your glasses!

I must make a note of this.

So? I hate reading anyway.

"Behaviour may be an important indicator of an underlying problem."

Individual Education Plan

Name of Pupil __Billy Blunt__   Date of Birth __16.4.99__   Class __Year 4__

Concern	Target	Criteria for success	Provision/Resources	Personnel
Sight Vocabulary	To know 10 high-frequency words: went, it's, from, children, just, help, don't, old, by, time	To recognise the words in and out of context on 3 separate occasions	Easylearn: Out of Sight flash cards/games 1 hour per week Precision teaching: 5 minutes daily	Miss Scott (TA) Mrs Blunt (Parent)
Spelling	To spell 10 high-frequency words: said, have, like, some, come, were, there, little, one, when	To spell the words correctly and unaided on 3 separate occasions	Look, say, cover, write, check method 10 minutes daily	Sally Smith (pupil: Billy's spelling buddy)
Writing	To be able to write one correctly constructed sentence independently	To accomplish this on 3 separate occasions	Daily diary / one sentence a day Easylearn: Simple Sentences LML: Writing Sentences, book 1 30 mins per week	Miss Scott (TA)
Phonics	To be able to cvc blend using medial 'a'	To be able to read and sound out cvc words in and out of context, to include nonsense words	Easylearn: Phonics book 2 LML: New Phonic Blending: tape 2 LDA: Paper Chains Phonics: set 1 90 mins per week	Miss Scott (TA)

Date of Plan __10 Sept__   Date of Review __12 Dec__   Parent's Signature __C Blunt__

Teacher's Signature __L Green__   Name of TA __Mandy Scott__   Provision __3 hours per week__

Record of work for pupils with IEPs

Record of work for a pupil with an Individual Education Plan

To be completed by Teaching Assistant

Date/Time	Activity	Skills	Observations	Staff
Sept 9 9.00 – 10.00	Phonic Blending Tape 1. Lesson 3. cvc blending (group)	Phonics	Billy enjoyed this activity and was able to sound out, and build up all the words on his own (forgot glasses).	M Scott
Sep 15 9.00 – 9.30	Write a sentence in his diary. Page 3 Easylearn: Simple Sentences (1:1)	Sentence construction	Still forgets to begin sentences with a capital letter. Needs lots more practice.	M Scott
Sep 16 9.00 – 10.00	Matching pairs game using flash cards. Easylearn – Out of Sight pages 4 & 5 (group)	Sight vocabulary	Billy has remembered the five words learned last week: will introduce the next five tomorrow (forgot glasses again!)	M Scott
Sep 17 9.30 – 10.00	CVC blending game LDA- Paper Chains Phonics: set 1 (1:1)	Phonics	Did really well – gave him a sticker. Starting to blend well. He read his words to Miss Green (still no glasses – Miss Green will send a letter home).	M Scott

Pupil's name ___Billy Blunt___   Class ___Year 4___   TA's name ___Mandy Scott___   Hours per week ___3___

Record of work for pupils with IEPs

Record of work for a pupil with an Individual Education Plan

To be completed by Teaching Assistant

Date/Time	Activity	Skills	Observations	Staff

Pupil's name _____ Class _____ TA's name _____ Hours per week _____

Records and reviews

Review meetings

If part of your role is to support a child with SEN, you should be invited to attend the review meetings. These are usually held every term to discuss the progress of pupils towards achieving their IEP targets. Your part in these meetings is important, although sometimes it may be difficult for you to attend (they may be held after school at a time when you are not paid to be there). You may be asked to prepare a brief written report if you do not attend. It is particularly important that you attend reviews if you are supporting a child with a statement. Some schools pay TAs a fee for attending reviews held after the official school day.

School Action reviews: It is likely that the class teacher, SENCo and parents will attend. These pupils do not usually have the support of a TA. It is at these meetings that a decision may be taken to move a pupil on to School Action Plus.

School Action Plus reviews: Reviews will include a visiting professional, and it is more likely that a TA will be involved. If so, you will be expected to provide a report on the work you are doing with the child. If you are unable to attend, you may be asked to give a written report to the SENCo in order to provide your feedback on the pupil's progress. The outcome of these meetings may be to request the LA to make a statutory assessment of the pupil's needs, with the hope that the LA will provide the pupil with the protection of a statement.

Review meetings for pupils with statements: These are statutory reviews and more formal than other reviews. They are usually held once a year. Anybody involved in the provision of care for the child – the parent; SENCo; head teacher; class teacher; TA; professionals from outside organisations such as the educational psychologist, speech and language therapist or physiotherapist; and the LA officer responsible for SEN – will be invited to attend. Each person provides a written report two weeks before the review date, which is then circulated to all involved.

The meeting: The head teacher usually leads the meeting. The child is not usually at the review, but their views will have been recorded before the meeting and are taken into account. After that there will be a general discussion of the current provision, during which any recommendation for change is made. The meeting may decide the pupil needs more or less TA time, or the intervention of a different professional. Very occasionally, the LA may decide the best future for the pupil is in a special school. It is the SENCo's job to fill in the forms following the meeting to document all that has happened, and send them to the LA.

You may find the idea of writing a report daunting, but you will be given lots of guidance. Your input will be highly valued as you will be one of the people working closely with the pupil. The example on page 49 is a useful guide to the kind of information needed in such a report. On page 50 there is a blank sheet

If you want happiness for an hour, take a nap. If you want happiness for a day, go fishing. If you want happiness for a year, inherit a house. If you want happiness for a lifetime, help someone.

(Chinese proverb)

Review Meeting Report

Name of Child __Billy Blunt__   Date of Birth __16.4.99__   Class __Year 4__

Name of Teaching Assistant __Mandy Scott__

Provision __3 hours per week (1 hour 1:1, 2 hours group work)__

Date of Review __2nd July__

....

IEP Target   Reading.   To know 10 high-frequency words

Comments   Billy knows 6/10 words. He does not know: children, help, don't, time.

....

IEP Target   Spelling.   To spell 10 high-frequency words

Comments   Billy can spell 8/10 words. He cannot spell: little, when.

....

IEP Target   Writing.   To be able to write one sentence independently

Comments   Billy is able to write a sentence on his own which begins with a capital letter and ends with a full stop.

....

IEP Target   Phonics.   To be able to blend 3-letter words with medial 'a'

Comments   Billy is now able to blend any 3-letter word using a, e, i, o and u.

....

Additional Targets

Comments   Billy's target to remember his glasses every day has not been achieved.

....

What has been positive about the support?

Billy enjoys the sessions and is beginning to build up good relationships with the other children in the group. He is becoming more confident and starting to put his hand up in class.

Is there anything you would like to change regarding the nature of the support?

Yes, Billy prefers working in a group and does not need 1:1 support now, so I think he should work 3 hours in a group.

What are the child's views regarding the work carried out with you?

Billy enjoys working with me, but not when we are on our own together. He says he feels like a baby. He is beginning to be reluctant to leave the rest of the class.

Do you have any further comments?

I am very pleased with Billy's progress but he still finds remembering words to read and spell very difficult.

Signed __Mandy Scott__   Date __2 July__

Permission to Photocopy

Review Meeting Report

Name of Child _____ Date of Birth _____ Class _____

Name of Teaching Assistant _____

Provision _____

Date of Review _____

....

IEP Target

Comments

....

IEP Target

Comments

....

IEP Target

Comments

....

IEP Target

Comments

....

Additional Targets

Comments

....

What has been positive about the support?   What are the child's views regarding the
                                                  work carried out with you?

Is there anything you would like to change   Do you have any further comments?
regarding the nature of the support?

Signed _____   Date _____

which you may use in preparation for your report; your school may have its own pro forma for you to use instead.

Areas of difficulty

If your TA job involves you in working with a child with a particular SEN, the school should provide you with detailed information on the condition as well as on what is required of you to support the child. There are many factors in an SEN. These include the severity and complexity of the need, home circumstances, the quality of teaching, resources and support in school and, of course, the effectiveness of the TA.

The 2002 Code identifies four main areas of SEN:

- cognition and learning difficulties
- emotional, behavioural and social difficulties
- communication and interaction difficulties
- sensory and/or physical difficulties.

A pupil may have problems in more than one area.

Cognition and learning difficulties
General learning difficulties

These pupils are likely to show:

- low levels of attainment in all forms of assessment including, for younger children, baseline assessments;
- difficulty in acquiring skills (notably in literacy and numeracy) on which much other learning in school depends;
- difficulty in dealing with abstract ideas and generalising from experience;
- a range of associated difficulties, notably in speech and language (particularly for younger children) and in social and emotional development.

Case study

Usma works with Joe, a pupil with a statement, for three hours a week. He has been assessed as having general learning difficulties. Joe is a Year-4 pupil aged 9, and his level of understanding in literacy and numeracy is what would be expected from a pupil in Year 1.

Usma's time is mainly spent supporting Joe in class during literacy and numeracy sessions. For one half-hour session a week, Usma works in a one-to-one situation with Joe, supporting him by working towards the five targets on his IEP. Today the target is to spell ten of the high frequency words. He has to copy the selected word correctly from the whiteboard by putting plastic letters into the correct order and then writing the word in his book. For another half-hour she works with him in a small group experiencing similar difficulties. The work focuses on the development of phonics, spelling and writing skills, using a variety of resources.

The educational psychologist is also involved with Joe and visits him every month to assess his progress and offer advice and support to the school. The programme of work carried out by Usma is reflected in the teacher's planning.

Specific learning difficulties

Some pupils will experience difficulties with learning in specific areas. These pupils may be found to have dyslexia or dyspraxia. They are likely to have problems in one or more of the following areas:

- fine or gross motor skills;
- low attainment in one or more curriculum areas, particularly when this can be traced to difficulties in underlying literacy and/or numeracy skills;
- inconsistency in attainment (e.g. better oral than written work);
- signs of frustration and/or low self-esteem, sometimes taking the form of behavioural difficulties;
- tasks involving specific skills such as sequencing and organisation, or phonological or short-term memory abilities;
- in younger children, limited skills in verbal exchanges or in following instructions; delays in forming concepts, especially when information requires first-hand sensory experience.

It is always hard when you feel really pleased with how well a pupil has come on, and then you realise how big the gap is between her and the rest of the class. It seems sometimes that whatever you do will never be good enough.

Case study

Karen works with Gemma, who has been assessed as having dyslexia. Gemma is a very bright and articulate pupil but she experiences great problems with reading and spelling, which are leading to a sense of frustration and a deterioration in her behaviour. The advice on her IEP came from a specialist visiting teacher, who has trained Karen to deliver a programme of work called Toe by Toe devised to support Gemma. Karen works with Gemma for 1½ hours per week in a 1:1 situation delivering the programme. She meets with the SENCo once a week, when she is able to discuss Gemma's progress.

Emotional, behavioural and social difficulties

Pupils experiencing these difficulties are likely to show:

- age-inappropriate behaviour or behaviour that seems otherwise inappropriate or strange;
- behaviour that interferes with the learning of the pupil or their peers, such as persistent calling out in class, refusal to work, or annoyance of peers;
- signs of emotional turbulence, such as unusual tearfulness or withdrawal from social situations;
- difficulties in forming and maintaining positive relationships, such as isolation from peers or aggression towards peers or adults.

Too much noise in the classroom when I am working with my SEN pupil – he gets distracted, but I am not allowed to take him out.

Case study

Pat supports Della, a Year-8 pupil who has emotional and behavioural difficulties. Della finds it impossible to concentrate in the classroom and often refuses to work. She also leaves the classroom without permission and has been involved in some violent incidents with other pupils. Della has a statement giving her seven hours of TA provision a week, five hours in the classroom, where Pat ensures Della stays on task. Pat spends one hour 1:1 with Della working on targets set in the IEP. One of the targets is to complete the agreed amount of work. For example, today Della has agreed to complete ten sentences from a worksheet by the end of the literacy session. The remaining hour is spent in a small group to help Della build social and relationship skills. Pat works with Della to improve her low self-esteem throughout.

Communication and interaction difficulties
Speech and language difficulties

Pupils in this category are likely to have difficulty in the following areas:

- the production of speech;
- finding words and joining them together in meaningful and expressive language;
- communicating through speech and other forms of language;
- understanding or responding to the verbal cues of others;
- the acquisition and expression of thoughts and ideas;
- understanding and using appropriate social language;
- frustration and anxieties arising from a failure to communicate, possibly leading to apparent behavioural difficulties and deteriorating social and peer relationships.

The room I work in is the library and there are always pupils coming in and out disturbing us.

Case study

Marlon, a Year-2 pupil, has been placed on School Action Plus because he has severe speech problems and it is very difficult for anyone to understand what he is saying. He has the support of a TA, Adrian, for three hours a week. Adrian has received specific training and guidance from a speech and language therapist, who visits him every six weeks to discuss the effectiveness of the programme with him, the class teacher and the SENCo. The IEP indicates very clear guidelines, teaching strategies and resources. Adrian's role is to deliver a language development programme devised by the speech therapist. Today Marlon is looking at pictures which begin with the sounds he finds difficult: sh, fr and fl. He has to say two sentences about each one. Adrian repeats his sentences correctly and then Marlon has to copy them.

Autistic spectrum disorders

Pupils with ASD may have difficulty with social relationships, social communication and imaginative thought. They may show:

- difficulties in attuning to social situations and responding to normal environmental cues;
- evidence of emerging personal agendas that are increasingly not amenable to adult direction;
- a tendency to withdraw from social situations and increasing passivity and absence of initiative;
- repressed, reduced or inappropriate social interactions extending to highly egocentric behaviour with an absence of awareness of the needs and emotions of others;
- impaired use of language, either expressive or receptive – this may include odd intonation, forms and limited expression, reducing the potential for two-way communication;
- limitations in expressive or creative peer activities, extending to obsessive interests or repetitive activities.

I need to spend more time with my pupil, as she would make a lot more progress. She cannot manage in the classroom on her own.

Case study

Alice works with Sadie, a Year-9 pupil, for ten hours a week. Sadie is autistic and has a statement. IEP targets are concerned with Sadie's emotional and learning difficulties, and are aimed at developing social skills. Most work takes place in a small group as Sadie finds it difficult to cope in the classroom situation. By encouraging Sadie to interact with others in the group, it is hoped to help her understand the unwritten rules of socialising and to build effective relationships with her classmates. For example, today she is learning about waiting her turn – by putting up her hand to answer questions. She will practise this when Alice is not around and will be monitored by the teacher, who will feed back to Alice.

Sensory and physical difficulties

Hearing impairment

These pupils' problems will range from mild to severe and present in the following ways:

- deterioration in academic performance, such as handwriting, speech, lack of response to verbal cues or increasing requests for repetition of instructions;

- physical changes such as persistent discharge from the ears, tilting of the head to hear better, or a need to focus on the teacher's face when instructions are given;

- increased reliance on classmates to relay or clarify instructions;

- frustration with themselves or with others for no apparent reason, leading to emotional or behavioural problems.

Case study

Sally works with Parvinder, in Year 6, who has a statement for five hours a week. He has significant hearing loss and wears a hearing aid. Parvinder has learning difficulties and problems in forming relationships with other children. Sally follows IEP targets and regularly meets with the Hearing Impaired Service. She also works on Parvinder's low self-esteem to help him build relationships with his peers. Some support is on a 1:1 basis, and for three hours a week he works in a small group.

Visual impairment

The indicators for this category are:

- possible deterioration in handwriting, slowness in copying from the board, asking for written instructions to be given verbally;

- deterioration in hand–eye coordination, excessive straining of the eyes to read the board, needing to be at the front of the class to see the TV or pictures in books, etc.;

- anxiety in performing certain physical activities in PE or in moving around the playground;

- evidence of stress leading to withdrawn or frustrated behaviour.

Su-Yen works with Pete, a Year-10 pupil who has a statement owing to deteriorating sight. This has led to limited progress in learning tasks and a consequent loss of confidence. Books of normal print size are difficult for Pete to read. His IEP includes the use of low-vision aids like a raised desktop and a special magnifying glass. Su-Yen also makes enlarged photocopies of worksheets for him.

I like the feeling I have when I see children's faces light up when I go to the class to collect them.

Physical and medical difficulties

Only pupils whose medical or physical conditions prevent them accessing the curriculum, thereby creating an SEN, should be included here. Conditions to look out for include:

- evidence of a learning difficulty;
- disability that affects the pupil's confidence, self-esteem, emotional stability or relationship with peers;
- disability that has an impact on classroom performance because of lack of concentration, drowsiness or lack of motivation;
- disability that affects performance in other areas of the curriculum, such as PE.

Jane works with Leila from Year 2 for two hours a week. Her needs are met through School Action Plus, as last year she lost the use of her right hand in an accident. The school developed a programme in consultation with an occupational therapist, who also advised on equipment. Leila has made good progress, and her confidence is growing. It is expected that one day she will not require any support.

Sometimes our light goes out but is blown into flame by another human being. Each of us owes our deepest thanks to those who have rekindled the light.

Albert Schweitzer

From these glimpses into real-life scenarios you can see how much difference an effective TA can make to a child with an SEN. The TA's role is often to minimise difficulties by differentiating the curriculum to ensure pupil participation as far as possible, and to support the child in becoming as independent as they can be. Knowledge of the difficulty is obviously important, as is knowing how best to help the pupil at a practical level in the classroom. To me, though, the most important aspects of the TA–pupil relationship are the TA's ability to communicate effectively with the pupil, to raise their self-esteem and confidence and to help them accept and come to terms with their disability. How rewarding it is to think that because of your input, you have helped a child go forward into their life better able to cope.

I just need to finish this chapter...

Can I have my book back now?

STAFF ROOM

Chapter 6
Working with the school and staff

Working as a TA gives you the opportunity to extend your own knowledge in many areas: understanding how children learn, knowing how best to work with pupils with SEN, discovering children's authors whom you love reading, acquiring interesting historical facts. For the first time, you may even learn how to do long division! Another great advantage is that the job involves working closely with others and close working relationships are rewarding. You will be working alongside lots of different adults within the school environment, including the senior management team, class teachers, other TAs, parents and visiting professionals. You will be able to do your job much more easily and effectively if you build up good working relationships with them. Sometimes, through no fault of your own, this can be a real challenge. This chapter will tell you what to expect from the school and your class teacher, as well as what to do if things are not working as well as they should.

Support for you
The school
As a TA you have certain responsibilities, as outlined in Chapter 3. The school also has responsibilities towards you. These include:

- considering your skills and interests and placing you in the most appropriate classes;
- ensuring you receive regular training;
- having an effective induction programme in place;
- offering you opportunities to undertake appropriate qualifications;
- providing a regularly updated job description;
- providing regular appraisal;
- ensuring that you have a timetable clarifying where you will be working and the general structure of the school day.

The teacher
The class teacher you work with has responsibilities towards you as well:

- Involving you in planning lessons if possible, so you can have an input.
- Providing you with copies of plans in advance of lessons.
- Making sure the plans clarify what is expected of you during teaching sessions, such as:
  - providing general support to the whole class – this usually involves assisting with spellings, clarifying work for pupils, making suggestions, troubleshooting, and offering praise and reassurance;

- working with a group – the nature of the work you are to carry out, resources you will need, the learning objective;
- Informing you about how you should feed back to the teacher.
- Ensuring you have appropriate knowledge of the SEN pupils you are working with.
- Clarifying the work you need to carry out with a specific SEN pupil:
  - providing you with the IEP showing the pupil's targets;
  - talking you through the school SEN policy: a 'must read' document;
  - demonstrating what standard of work is expected and acceptable;
  - explaining what resources you will need and where they are located.
- Making you aware of your role regarding behaviour management:
  - what the school/classroom rules are;
  - what rewards and sanctions you may deliver;
  - what is in the behaviour policy – another piece of essential reading.
- Discussing the responsibility you have with regard to the health and safety of all pupils:
  - you will be expected to read the Health and Safety and the Equal Opportunities policies, which will set out the school's approach to protecting both the physical and emotional well-being of all pupils;
  - you should be able to recognise any risks in the school environment that may be the cause of potential incidents, such as leads from computers trailing across the floor;
  - understanding what a risk assessment is and when it needs to be carried out, for example when accompanying pupils on educational visits.
- Informing you of procedures which are in place to help pupils with spellings – consistency of approach is very important.
- Explaining the meaning of educational jargon. If you find a teacher referring to SATs, dyspraxia or cloze procedure and you don't fully understand what is meant, do ask.
- Arranging regular meetings with you to see how things are going as well as listening to your feedback regarding the pupils, and incorporating this into future lesson planning if possible.

If you work predominantly with one pupil in one class, their class teacher may be your line manager as well, in which case they will have a wider remit of responsibilities and should be the first port of call for any queries or concerns. They tend to deal also with appraisals or sick leave and so on. Alternatively, your line manager may be the SENCo, head teacher or another member of the senior management team.

A good working relationship

Many TAs work very closely and successfully with teachers, building up great relationships and becoming an entertaining and inspiring 'double act' in the classroom. If you aren't getting on particularly well with a teacher, it may help to look at the situation from their perspective. Imagine you do have a problem with a teacher – let's call her Mrs Bibby – who you feel undervalues your work,

He seems interested in what I have to say about the pupils.

He helped me when he heard a pupil cheeking me, not in a way I found embarrassing and patronising but in a supportive way, if you know what I mean.

Teachers sometimes talk and use jargon I don't understand. It makes me feel stupid.

She treats me like a human being and always asked how my husband was when he was in hospital.

I don't like it when the teacher keeps leaving the room, leaving me to cope on my own each time. I don't like the responsibility.

doesn't include you in lessons and doesn't manage her class well, which makes your job more difficult. It may be that Mrs Bibby lacks confidence herself and feels intimidated by your presence in class, but her pride prevents her from asking for help. She may have other personal problems which are affecting her work.

Being aware of this should help you to understand her better and to improve your working relationship. Don't just assume the problem is down to you. Many teachers are not trained as managers, and may find it difficult to be suddenly responsible for managing another adult in the classroom. If problems persist, it is far better to try to resolve the issue directly than to say nothing and allow problems to escalate. Issues often arise due to miscommunication or misinterpretation of someone else's behaviour. If the situation doesn't improve, you may need to approach your line manager or a senior member of staff for support. In addition, you may want to join a union in case you find yourself with a grievance that the school is not able to resolve.

What do I do when ...?

Communication is definitely the key to trouble-shooting any problems that arise, specifically seeking support and advice from more experienced colleagues. A list of problem-solving tips appears below.

Scenario	Problem-solving
I feel the teacher doesn't know what to do with me and I just sit there in lessons not doing much.	Talk to the teacher and explain the situation. They may not be aware of how you feel. You could suggest to them ways you could help, or pupils you feel would benefit from working with you.
I never seem to get the chance to talk to the teacher or to feed back about pupils' progress in lessons.	Ask the teacher if it would be possible to have a brief discussion each day; five minutes in the classroom before the children come into school can be invaluable, followed by five minutes at the end of the day. Or you could complete written feedback daily, and meet weekly to discuss it.
All the work the teacher provides for the statemented pupil I work with is far too difficult.	Talk to the SENCo, who will communicate with the teacher on your behalf; you and the teacher should be shown more appropriate resources.
I never seem to be given a copy of the class plans in advance, so I don't know what subject or topic we will be working on.	Ask the teacher if they can put a copy of the plans in your pigeon-hole every week – or whatever is feasible. Explain that you feel unprepared and this affects your work with the children.

Scenario	Problem-solving
I don't get enough help with badly behaved children in my group. I don't know how to manage their behaviour.	Discuss the issue and ask for further strategies you could use, or involve the teacher with monitoring the behaviour. For example, explain to pupils at the beginning of the session that if they misbehave they will go back to the class and the teacher will apply the sanction. Some pupils may not be suitable for your group; don't be afraid to say so.
I never seem to get any training. I don't feel equipped to deal with the children I work with.	Find out from the senior management team what the policy towards training is. Schools may have a training budget which should be equally shared amongst TAs. Sometimes, instead of training, it is valuable to visit a school to observe another TA working with a pupil similar to one with whom you are experiencing problems.

Communication and reporting back

It's often not possible to speak to a teacher immediately following a session. Written reports can be easier and more reliable. Group record forms are different from those considered in the previous chapter, which focus specifically on one pupil's progress towards their IEP targets. Group record forms can be used with any pupils you are working with to record the work they have done in a particular session. A lot of schools have their own forms for reporting back, but it will be useful for you to have an idea of the type of records which may be expected. An example of a completed group record sheet is shown on page 60. There is also a blank template on page 61 for you to use for group observations if you wish. Some schools may ask you to annotate a copy of the teacher's planning sheet with brief notes on what each pupil has achieved. An example of this is on page 62. Whatever format they follow, your records will inform teachers' planning as well as documenting the work you have done.

Induction, reviews and appraisals

When you start your new job you should have a settling-in period. Schools have often developed a routine for introducing TAs to their new role. A week of preparation or induction is desirable. During this time you should be able to:

- meet and observe TAs at work;
- find out about the layout of the school and where the resources are kept;
- meet the teachers with whom you will be working;
- study lesson plans so you understand their format and how they include TAs;
- read a selection of books for TAs, if your school has these;

She always reads the reports I write, and always tells me what has happened in the planning meeting. The staff meetings are after school and I do not have to go, but the teacher always tells me what has happened.

Group record: TA feedback sheet

Class ___2G___   (Literacy)/ Numeracy

Teacher ___Mrs Gilbert___

Teaching Assistant ___Miss Potter___   Date ___June 9___

To be completed by the teacher before the lesson or TA at start of lesson.

Objective: to reinforce cvc work; to be able to recognise cvc words with medial a.

Activity: with the Green group (6 pupils)

To play a cvc game using magnetic letters and board. Each pupil has 10 letters, with 'a' as the only vowel. Each child puts their letters on to the board when they have found a word, and all the group then copy the words into My Phonics Book. Title at top of the page: My Words!

Extension activity: pupils who finish 6 words can choose two words to draw and label.

Equipment:

6 sets of magnetic letters (remove e i o u)

magnetic whiteboard

pencils

crayons

To be completed by the Teaching Assistant during the lesson.

Name	Comment	Was objective achieved?
Robert	Tried very hard but does not know s, b or d so found it hard to make up words.	No. Needs further reinforcement.
Simone	Completed quickly and easily.	Yes. Ready to move on to medial e.
Fayed	Forgot his glasses and seemed very tired. Did not complete the work, although he seems to know all the sounds.	No. Needs further reinforcement.
Oliver	Did very well. Had the time to draw pictures for all 6 words.	Yes. Ready to move on to medial e.
Ella	Completed quickly and easily.	Yes. Ready to move on to medial e.
Deborah	Seemed to have forgotten all she learned last time. Only recognised c, a and m.	No. Needs further reinforcement.

General comment

The group now needs to be split into two, with two different lots of work.

Group 1: Ella, Oliver and Simone need to move onto medial e.

Group 2: Robert, Fayed and Deborah need more practice with individual letters.

Group record: TA feedback sheet

Class _____   Literacy / Numeracy

Teacher _____

Teaching Assistant _____ Date _____

To be completed by the teacher before the lesson or TA at start of lesson.

Objective:

Activity:

Equipment:

To be completed by the Teaching Assistant during the lesson.

Name	Comment	Was objective achieved?

General comment

Key Stage 3 planning sheet

Key Stage 3 planning sheet for Literacy: Twelfth Night

Look at website before the lesson to understand basic plot for Twelfth Night. http://www.channel4.com/learning/microsites/W/waywithwords/main.html

Date and lesson objective	Whole-class starter	Relevant student IEP targets	Word/sentence level work and handwriting	Activities	Plenary and self-assessment	Resources
Monday 20th November To develop understanding of characters (Viola and Sebastian) in the play.	THRASS alphabet rap and vowel phoneme – 6 sounds. Show the opening of the video 'Animated Tales' to see Viola and Sebastian.	<u>Group 1</u> Sarah – To copy handwriting patterns John – Go from left to right when making regular patterns to marks to represent writing <u>Group 2</u> Aisha – To form recognisable letters correctly Andrew – To talk about what he has read to show the development of precise understanding Nathan – To recount the main facts with support	<u>Group 1</u> – Teacher lead – Use chunky crayons to copy handwriting pattern ccccc <u>Group 2</u> – TA (Luke) lead – Rehearse the first join on Nelson sheet, use whiteboards to demonstrate and practise the join	<u>Group 1</u> – Teacher lead – To read words and recognise signs to describe Viola and Sebastian; boy, girl, twins, boat, fell off, lost each other. Match word to symbol. <u>Group 2</u> – TA (Luke) lead – Identify statements about Viola and Sebastian (from a selection of statements about other characters) to collect information about them.	<u>Teacher lead</u> Whole-class plenary in a circle – What do we know about Viola and Sebastian? Play a game where we guess the character. <u>TA</u> – Use plenary session to annotate work and write comments on lesson plan to feed back to teacher.	Animated Tales Video of Twelfth Night. <u>Group 1</u> Chunky crayons. 'C' template to write over. Enlarged images of Viola and Sebastian. Symbols and words for V and C. <u>Group 2</u> Nelson sheets. Statements about characters and chart to stick on to.

Monday records:

Luke's notes

<u>Activity 1</u> – all pupils completed the handwriting worksheet independently. The correct way to join letters was demonstrated to the pupils and they managed to copy correctly. They formed recognisable letters.

<u>Activity 2</u> – Some pupils initially found it difficult to read and understand quotes from the book. With verbal support all pupils managed to match quotes to the correct character. Nathan managed to sort quotes independently and showed understanding of characters and plot. All pupils were able to recall the main facts with some support.

○ familiarise yourself with the school polices, such as those on behaviour, health and safety, SEN and equal opportunities;

○ be made aware of your role regarding the school's child protection policy and procedures – you will need to look out for and report any signs of possible neglect, abuse or bullying and know the identity of the member of staff to whom you should report any concerns.

Your work should be reviewed regularly by your immediate line manager. Some TAs meet weekly with them, others once a term – it will depend on time constraints and the role you serve in school. These meetings are valuable as they give your line manager an opportunity to feed back to you, offer you praise and encouragement and perhaps discuss areas where there is room for development. They are also a chance for you to raise any concerns you have and discuss your feelings about the job.

I never seem to have enough time to talk to the teachers and some teachers never ask me how I have got on anyway.

You may receive an annual appraisal of your role from a member of the senior management team. Teachers always receive an annual appraisal, and some schools have a similar procedure for their TAs. That would involve discussing your personal situation and be likely to include the following aspects:

○ How do you feel about the job? What are the most/least enjoyable aspects?

○ How would you like to see your job develop over the next year?

○ What are your long-term career aspirations?

○ Are there are any training courses or qualifications you feel you would benefit from?

○ Do you have any concerns? Is there anything you need which is not provided for you at present?

If you are not given an opportunity to talk about these matters, it may be a good idea to consider them anyway and arrange a meeting with an appropriate person to discuss them.

The final word

I just love everything about my job and wouldn't change a thing. I feel so lucky.

I do hope you have found it helpful to read this book, and that you now feel equipped not only to survive but to succeed as a TA. It is a valuable and worthwhile job, that is also very rewarding, even if it is challenging at times! A chapter in this book has been devoted to training and qualifications. Of course that is important, but I should like to end with a quotation to get you thinking and to inspire you.

> *The key qualities of caring and empathy mean more in human relationships than any diplomas, degrees or technical skills.*

J. Canfield and H.C. Wells *100 Ways to Enhance Self-concept in the Classroom* (1994)

In other words, who you are is, in many ways, more important than what you do.

References

Birkett, V. (2004) *How to Support and Manage Teaching Assistants*. LDA: Cambridge

Canfield, J. and H.C. Wells (1994) *100 Ways to Enhance Self-concept in the Classroom*. Pearson Education: London

Department for Education and Skills (DfES) (2000) *Working with Teaching Assistants: A Good Practice Guide* (downloadable)

Department for Education and Skills (DfES) (2003) *Teaching Assistants File: Primary* (downloadable)

Department for Education and Skills (DfES) (2003) *Teaching Assistants File: Secondary* (downloadable)

Department for Education and Skills (DfES) (2007) *Letters and Sounds: Principles and Practice of High Quality Phonics* (downloadable, available in print in all schools)

Lawrence, D. (1996) *Enhancing Self-esteem in the Classroom*. Paul Chapman Publishing: London

National Foundation for Educational Research (NFER) (2007) *Research into the Impact of Support Staff Who Have Achieved HLTA Status*